CODHILL
Codhill Press Books

First Edition

Printed in the United States of America

Cover and interior book design by Graham Wood
cargocollective.com/grahamwoodwork

Library of Congress Cataloging-in-Publication Data
Names: Wood, Graham, 1965– author.
Title: Memory is the medium / Graham Wood.
Description: First edition. | New Paltz, NY : Codhill Press, 2017.
Identifiers: LCCN 2017046260 | ISBN 1930337957
Subjects: LCSH: Memory (Philosophy)—Miscellanea.
Classification: LCC BD181.7 .W66 2017 | DDC 128/.3—dc23
LC record available at https://lccn.loc.gov/2017046260

For Mira & Louis Wood "Second star on the right & straight on 'til morning."

Thanks to Kevin Slavin for the conversation
in the Irish pub in New York that Sunday night
when the words 'Memory is the Medium'
were conjured from the air

Thanks to William Charnock & Susannah Appelbaum

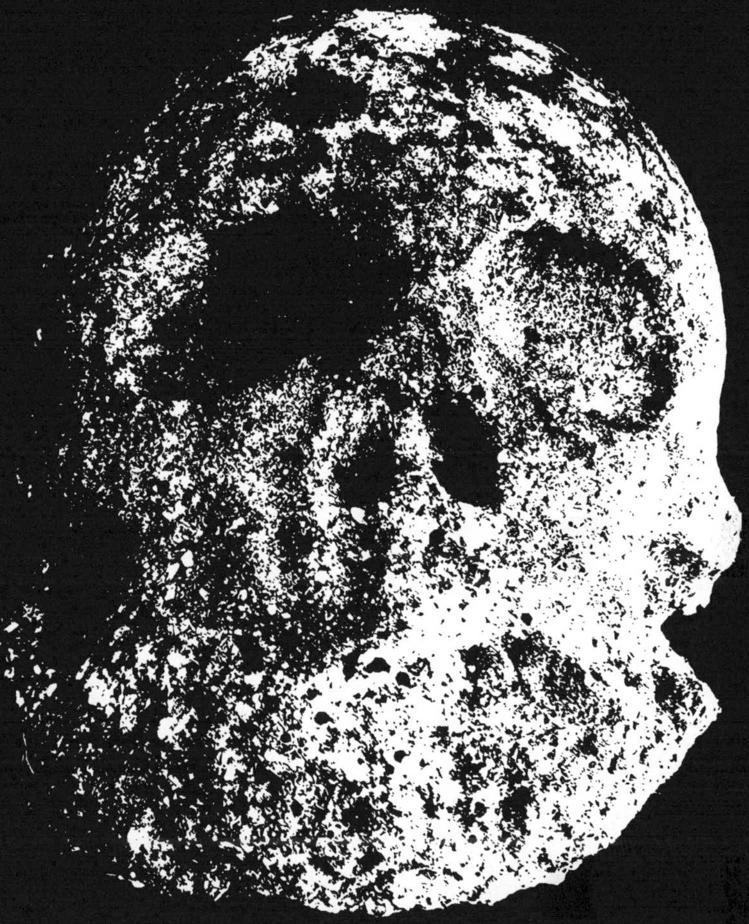

"Never let go of
that fiery sadness
called desire."
Patti Smith

Oscar Wilde is on trial and his friend George Ives begins a struggle that continues until this day: and the mountaineers and adventurers returned from the orient and south america as the 19th century turned, bringing with them transcendent stories and visions, symbols and signs of the micro- and macrocosmos; of harmony and mathematics and the body, the endless knot, the five wounds, the quarters, elementals reinterpreted, remade, remodelled, misunderstood and aggregated encompassing everything from anthropology to insanity and all that madness: rites and sects and signs and symbols without name or number (Buddhism and the Tao and the Tat Tvam Asi in all their forms as yet unknown to the west) inventive, impossible, prolific beyond measure they performed ritual, dreamed philosophical, played from dusk til golden dawn, enduring until

1) The idea of an idea

Sometimes in the still hours there's a wondering, a wandering from memory to possibility to presence and back, a driven drift idly

10) with unconditional love

focussed, attentive to
the chance that one
passing thing might
entice further
dreaming, a
mesmeric analysis of
its obverse,
edges and corners,
its unnoticed blemishes,
textures, microscopic flaws,
unfamiliar flavours, one
thing, another, this, this
. . . lapping, overlapping,
infusing, becoming . . .
summoning a memory,
or something just on the
tip of the tongue; then
it finds you as you find

it, simultaneously, a

subject,

an

THE FACT THAT IT'S AN IMPORTANT MEETING MEANS THE EXECUTIVE NEED NOT BE CONCERNED WITH ALL THOSE THINGS THAT ARE GOING ON TODAY.

object, a single thing or many all at once—it depends. It depends precisely on the particular thing that is wanting to be found at the moment you find it. That is, if it is true—if it is the thing that no matter what will see fruition even in spite of you. 'The idea' is something a bit soft but dangerous: a bit open, it demands and leads, is something inherent in actions, in passion, in sensation, in losing, in desperation, in experience, in understanding, in this now, in

this

is

this, in succumbing, in not being sure, in the beginning and the ending, in dreams . . . in casting doubt aside . . . An idea here is sort of, perhaps, almost anything—and the key here is to not pre-determine, to (almost) completely discard

THIS OUGHT TO BE A RELAXING FEELING.

preference, presumption and assumption and allow the process of working to determine the outcome. 'The idea' is something that is the heart of the reason that so many people do what they do, but it is something that exists just out of reach, fleeting and

elusive. It is the reason we

sing, write, make films,

the boulevards and avenues, invisible, disembodied, conjuring the coming century as an ecstatic aurora. To be modern! To be cosmic! To be ancient and magickal! The sounds and images, the words! A rite for spring, an uproar—Pschitt! A scandal! The Aeon of Horus has come! Abrahadabra! Imagination!

The prescient cry of the coming years, "Do what thou wilt shall be the whole of the law."

One year before the great war a woman steps in front of the King's horse at the Epsom Derby.

Magickal battles with former mentors, further expeditions beyond civilisation into unfamiliar desolate far distant lands, remote mountainous regions and mutiny, storm, death, and beyond, across the world, to a house in Scotland and an Abbey in Sicily, forming and reforming the process to transcendence through will and ether summoned visions of the universe, deeper and deeper into mystery unconscious, through experience and understanding while the wars roiled past reason, meaning become ash scattered through years, and space: and so these synapse-stars sparked

tell stories,
live and
breathe
and
find the
common
ground
between
each other;
and this reason is entirely
and specifically because
the 'idea' is multi-faceted,

fluid—it can be **an**
opinion, a

THE EXECUTIVE ALWAYS SEEMS RELAXED BUT ISN'T REALLY.

principle,
a method,
a notion,
a motif,
a theme,
a fancy, a
conception,
a flowering,
a surety,
an energy,
a fuel, a
memory, a

as Graves pursues
the possibility of
the White Goddess
of Birth, Love and
Death, the european
moon goddess in
whose honour all

medium.

An idea is something (and anything), and therefore not something: an idea is a thought that one has to make manifest and get out into the world unequivocally and unconditionally. It is not something that guarantees gain, reward, success.

. . . if you can do it all yourself in your own special way at the same time as others do their thing themselves in their own special way and you can find the best in those things equally letting go of understanding and expectation while fiercely playing as serious as life as momentary as the moment with every approach method pencil camera code mountain a possibility but really the singularity ahead forcing sight senses mind awake taking and using anymeansnecessary here's a chord here's a second

ESPECIALLY AT THE MOMENT.

here's a third now form
a band stealing thieving
finding sharing exchanging
overlaying travelling
returning talking seeking the
unrecognisable unfamiliar
unknown unexpected
manifesting phenomena
ritual conjuring meditative
repetition flow memory is
the medium holding the first
thought throughout while
its all finished already at the
beginning in your head as
you all weave along never
no always yes always total
fanatical sharing absolute
collaboration no hierarchy
no prestige in it together no
ego letting go of everything
but maintaining the essential
particular undiluted essence
the unique one time only its
all brand new the heart the
heart that's it there it's done
here it is now it is now and
then just stop it's a thing it's
made it's finished.

Then get it out in the world.

Then repeat.

Hitler's warlocks, a magickal symbol as foil to the swastika: he disseminated the sign through friends at the BBC and to

But different.

&

the same

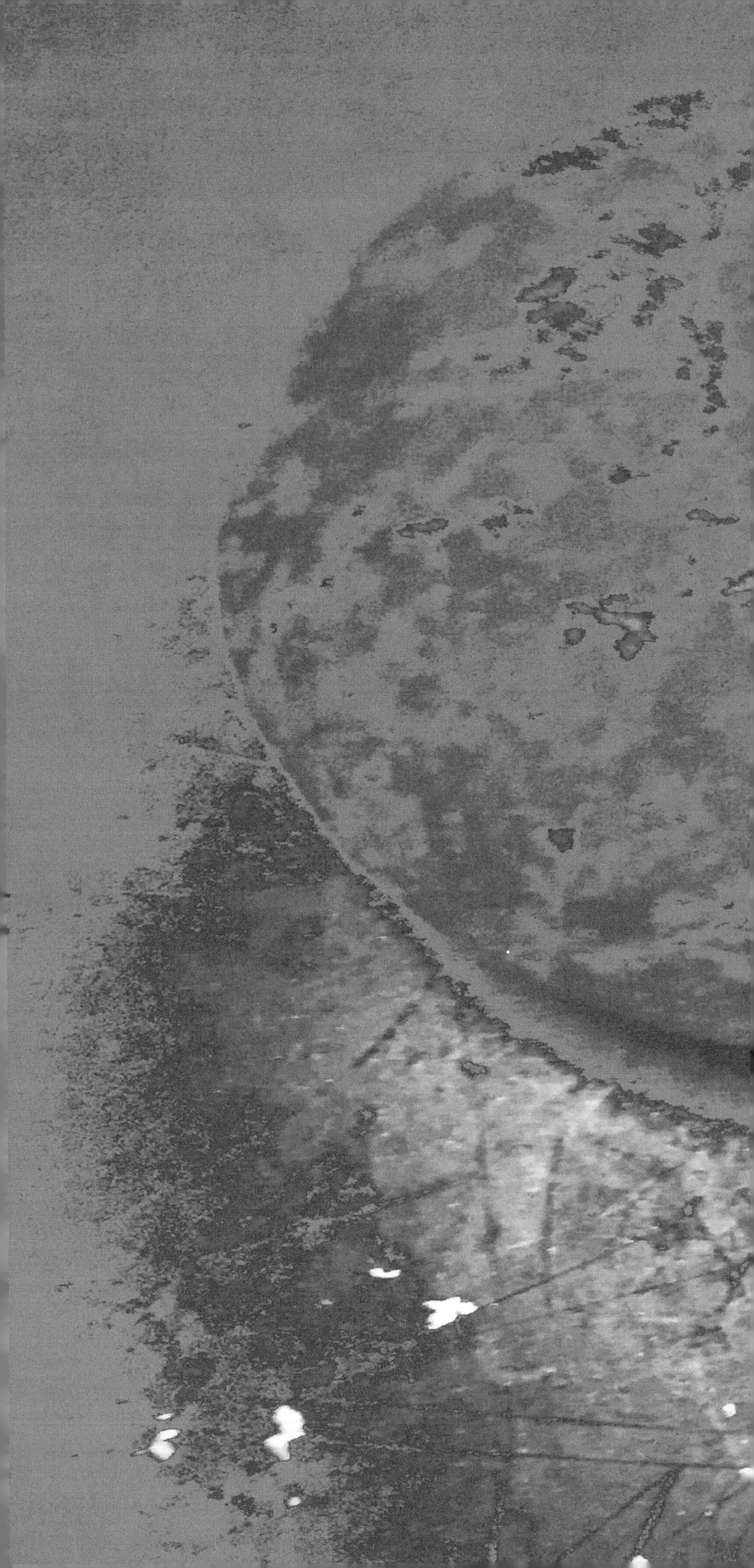

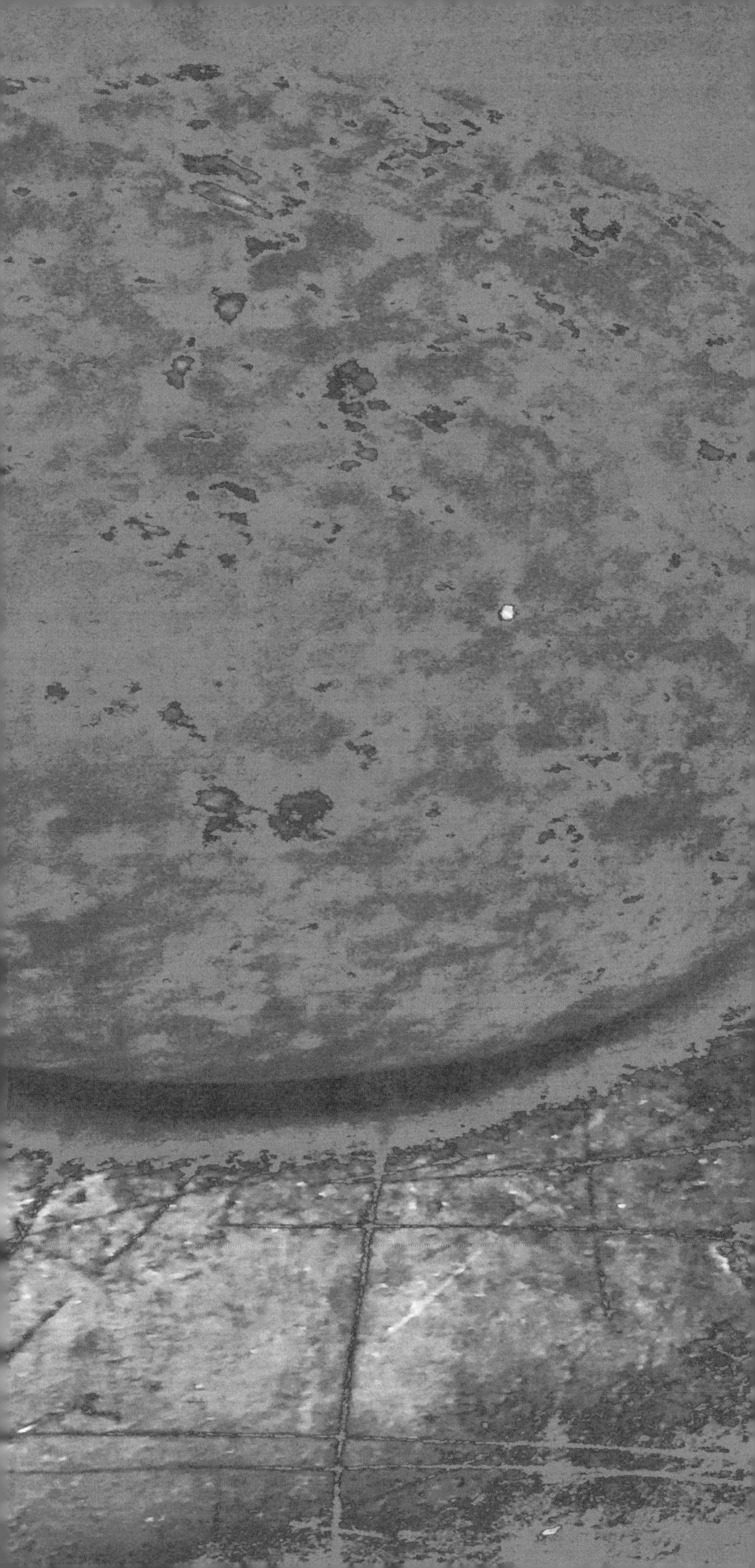

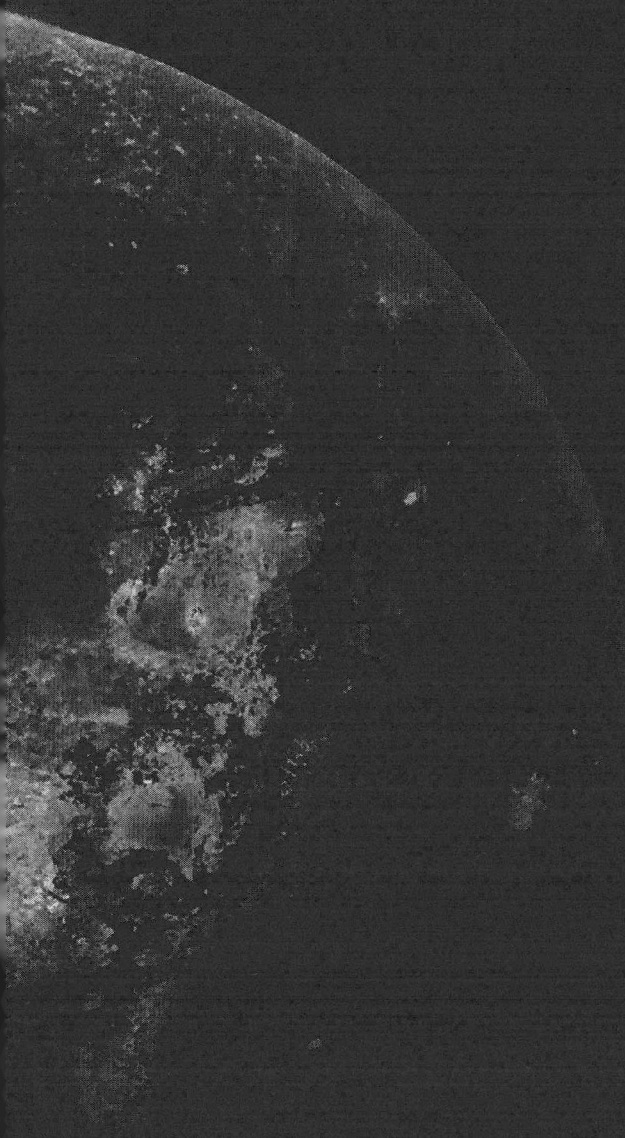

The Circle

The Salt
The Censer
The Candle
The Cup
The Bell
The Branch
The Knife
The Moon
The Forest

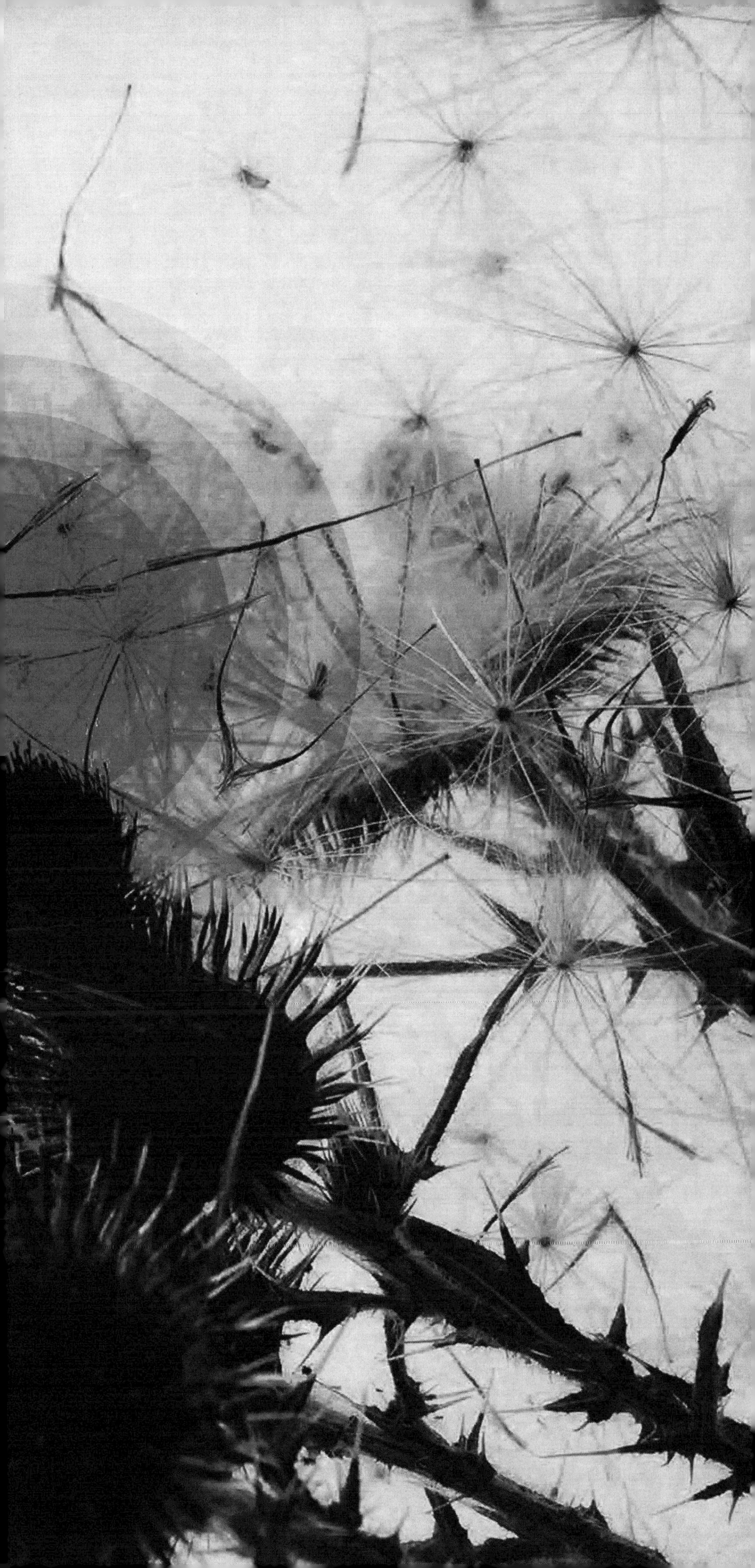

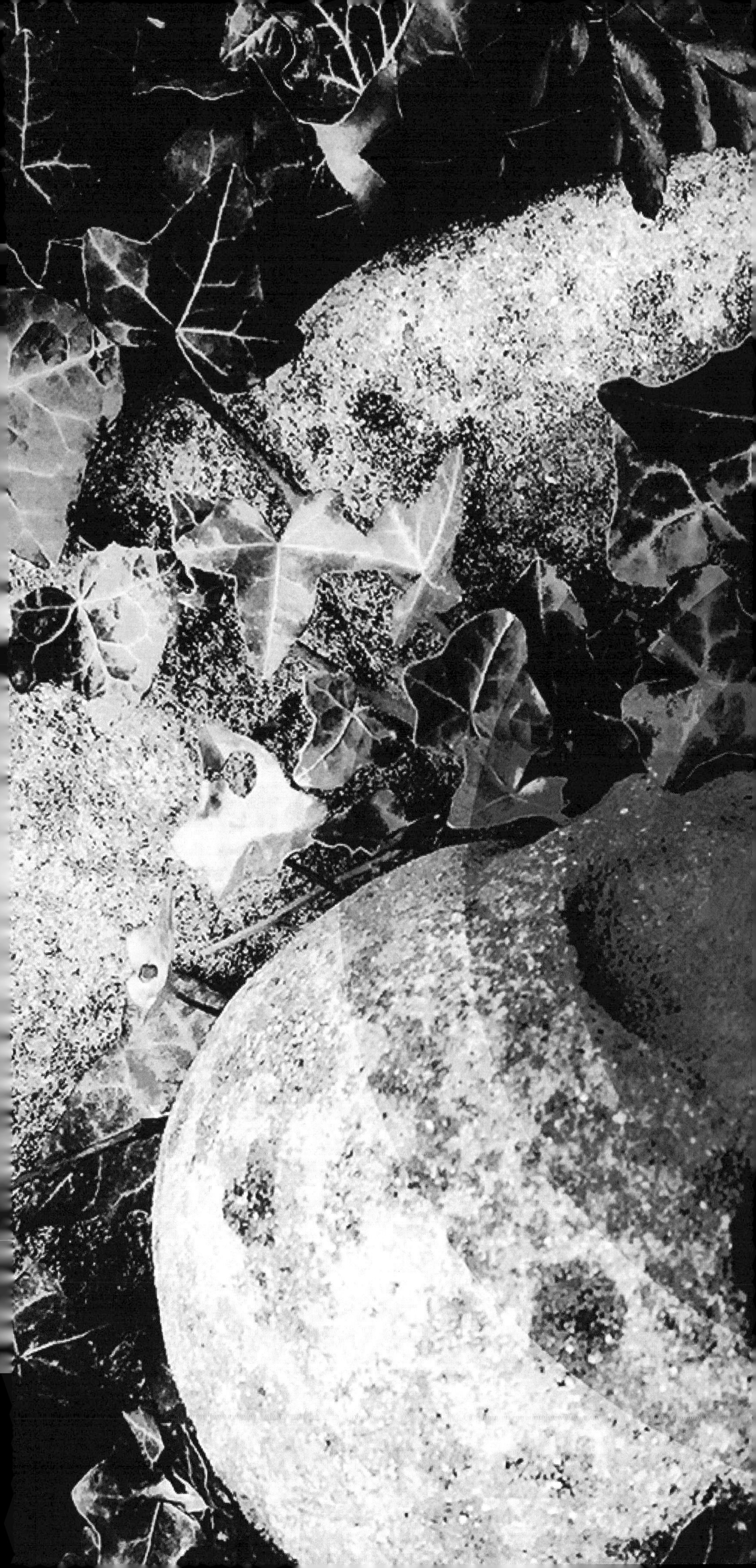

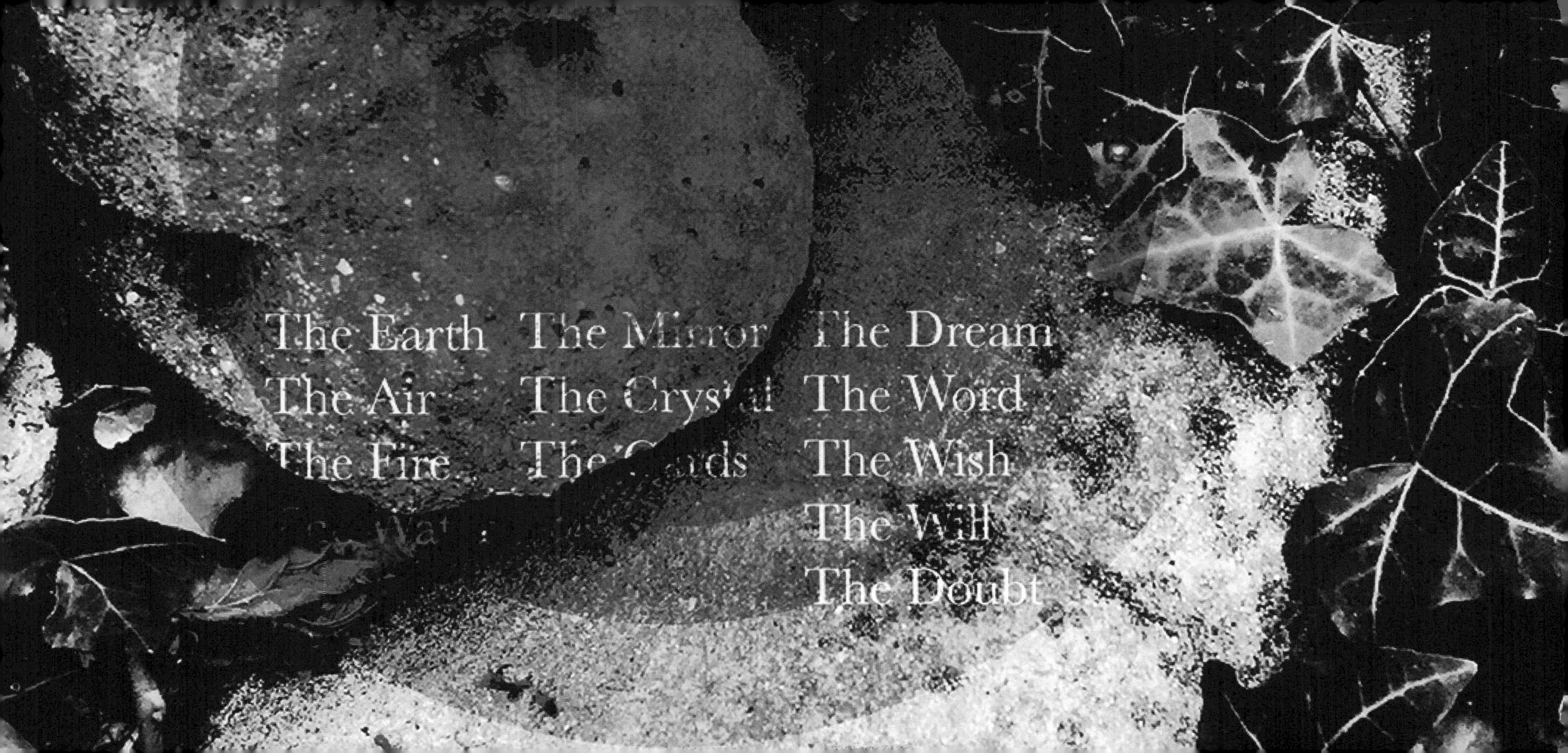
The Earth
The Air
The Fire
The Mirror
The Crystal
The Dream
The Word
The Wish
The Will
The Doubt

AUTUMN

**When autumn came in,
the days narrowed until there
was no sense of perspective,
no choices,
only now & what next.**

It is said we create our own realities,
and mine became one of postponement:
perception & assumption the cause
of a life of dwindling possibility.

Love remained;
and ambition & productivity.
I made things,

images & words & passing time.

My eyes are sore, red- crusted in the morning. I count the aches & remnants of injuries.
My shoulder. 10 years ago a dislocation, still not quite as strong
The left knee, a bad inversion 4 years ago. Now arthritic.
**A bit weeker than before. Right lower back. A pain i think from shifting boxes this week.
Makes me feel sick.**
I wonder. If you could swap minds with someone . . . if you could inhabit another body . .
would the shock of experiencing so immediately and so vividly their everyday aches & pains,
the injuries they bear from day to day almost without regard . . . would you go mad?

The sun, bright in the grey blue sky. The birds sing. Gulls. The estuary is near. River or sea?
Where one thing flows into another: change unseen, a merging.

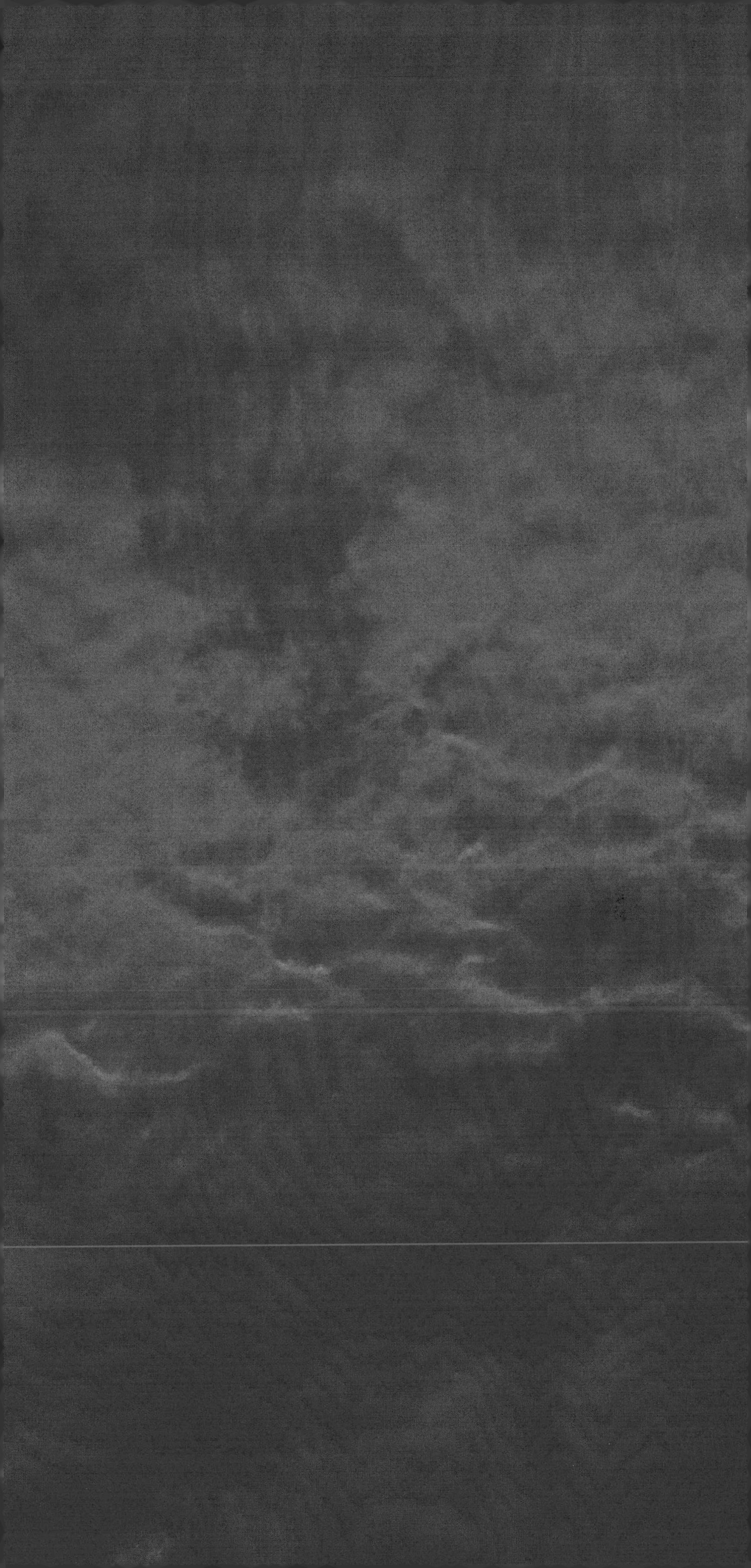

Now as the days go
down the sun haunts
the mornings in chill
air. Darkness overstays
and arrives unwanted,
early, but in-between
on occasion the blue
cold bright rips the
night open, shocked
immersion, low enough
to stretch shadows out
to the vanishing point.

The last fritillary clings
to the windowpane,
wings ragged,
phenomena, lost
sentinel of summer; a
remnant of childhood
fascination: a sign of
impending magic.

This season begets
witchcraft, conjuring

colours and light to
cast with: the incense
hanging sets the space
to draw the circle within
which passing through
portals to experience
and transformation and
bringing something
back, something that
broods and quietly
spreads, growing,
roots inside and waves
without, a strange
hybrid of spirit and
form, a creature that
speaks of things to feel,
to do, to make: a wild
impulse summoning
uncanny beauty to life.

We assume of others
that the plans they
conceive are driven like
our own: intentions,

ambitions, adorations,
frustrations. betrayals:
sacrifices. grey all day
today and in my head
as I drive is a song, a
ghost song, and words
turn over and over in
my mind: today we have
been driving all day and
it is grey. we rudderless
come about for then
and now and for ever
ever more: all of this has
happened before and it
will all happen again—
the push, the word,
the turn around, the
short step signed by the
flinty point marginally
shifted without, and will
not stop you know not
looking: momentarily
another second is empty
and is saved—and

distress and impulse;
then form, no form,
no impulse. no eyes
until no realm and no
extinction.

Now the rhythm has
gone for a time, I
think about the end
of the world, magic,
things like that, tracing
footsteps in tribute
to a story about love,
the end of the world,
magic, made by a man
who didn't know that
he was a real magician,
or that perhaps the end
of the world (change,
or at least his world)
would come sooner
than he thought. the
simplicity of following
a man, a character, who

finds his own path,
keeps to it, no matter
the consequence: ends
or means? what in
this appeals so much?
repels so much? then,
there's the quiet sound
of raindrops on the
windscreen, trucks
driving in the morning,
in those long, shifting,
floating dreams of
water and dirt, burnt
gold, fading light. she's
driving now: I wake
up, pick up my camera:
thinking of the man,
images on a screen
flickering, and I get out
of the car under this
bruised sky and wait
impatiently for her to
lock the doors, to get to
the old ruin.

A pebble beach,
yellow buoy, almost
cold, mostly grey,
and I wonder about
a thing- something
that is whole and
can be held perhaps,
comprehended, a
beginning a middle an
end- something like a
story (spasms, damage,
injury, almost recovery,
change), but that has
no end- is filled with
possibility, like the first
inkling of a thought,
communion, no-self,
flow, something always
different performed
in ritual circle, called,
conjured, scrying: a
crow, black and silent,
lands.

△

A stop.

Thinking of the Oort
Cloud. So far away. What
is its shape? In what
matter does it reside?
Thoughtfulness and
slow time. Reflection,
consideration. Study,
learning, understanding.
The long path. Questions
not easily answered.
Answers that give pause,
that require a response not
easily given, nor lightly.
Life faceted in curious
regard. To immerse in
fathoms dark, sounding.
To veer from the ecliptic
in oblique soaring.
Coagulation.

Hallucination
and delusion at

once entwined,
phantasmically
writhing, chimeras,
frenzy, hysteria,
dementia: an internal
derangement cast
catatonic across the
iris—throughout the
betraying hours of
ghast and limbo this
apparition clenches,
rictus human unmoving
envenomed in vein from
fist to knees rocking
haunching chanting
repeating unworded
again and over again
heels of palms rubbing
and rubbing the thighs;
unseeing eyes expanding
unwatered unblinking
even at the first ray: the
first day.

Shortening slowly
towards autumn:
summer still persists,
often stretching out
into the lengthening
shadows, a slow
dissipation into
September. How the
dog days remain longer
than expectation:
sometimes an Indian
heat the portal into
another season, turning,
this passing through . . .
always passing through:
a year, a month, a day,
an hour, from this to
this, from here to here,
from now to now.

Absent a line between:
out far so far far beyond
sounding fathoms,
no colour to describe

nor form to hold: a
limit unlimited and
liminal, faint glowing
from paledark to less: a
surface beneath which:
shifts and shades and
vibrations within,
under, through: all
these greys become
rubine. An error in the
vein; the trouble with
blood. When it clots.
Supernova. A twist in
the smile. Strange aches.
A story about feeling
better than before. How
the land stretches out
and away, fading from
house and house to
shape to line to grey.
How in this imaginary
thing (where there is
no centre only us) of
solidity and air there

is everything and more
there is healing.

We are our own portals;
we enter in and create
our space in time, in
memory, for ourselves
and each other, our
desires, our needs,
relationships; the
things we say and do,
the things we make.
These rituals—sleeping,
waking, remembering—
surround and infuse;
they emanate outwards,
encircling, overlapping.
Opening, stepping
through. Creating
openings, imagining
what could be in
between birth and
death, the entry and
the exit: what stands

between before and now: what was and is: where do we come from? Where are we going?

At first, and then . . . God? or Gods? or an explosion? or forever unfolding? or expanding and contracting? What cause, what effect? Things seem to begin and end—feel this moment to moment, a conversation, a walk, reading, a meal . . . a life. All things passing through.

At play as children we discover where things begin and end, and how in between we can

create space bounded
in order to explore,
to understand. Our
lives are a palimpsest
of human discovery;
the plain, the cave,
fire, magic, geometry,
alchemy, science and on,
all from one to another,
overlapping as we pass
through endeavour
ever onwards towards
another doorway.

Between the shore
and the sea is a white
temple that bridges one
experience and another
and each bridge between
is a ritual that awakens
another possibility.

Essentially repetition
creates ritual. The

processes of thinking and doing are built from experience through discovering what is within—a person's own ways of dealing with things—and what is without; the ways other people have done things before. Bridging, combining, colliding ways and means to create; to create a moment, a thing, a language, a world—to create anything. Building, drawing, writing, printing, photography, code, grids, narrative, editing, systems, process—all ritual to conjure portals to pass through into experience.

2) Memory is the medium

". . . every event in the visible world is the effect of an 'image', that is, of an idea in the unseen world. Accordingly, everything that happens on earth is only a reproduction, as it were, of an event in a world beyond our sense perception."

Richard Wilhelm, *Book of Changes*

Memory not only as "as many of the things i have experienced as possible until now, contained in what i sense as my mind" but also as the environment of everything from now and into the future-from-now: entering the memory to both affect the outside and also bring things out into the outside (the

Naval Intelligence and to MI5 until it gained Churchill's approval, a sigil that would endure and spread around the globe unlike any other. Crowley now engaged to work with the elite commando unit on the most crucial missions: meanwhile the new world burgeoned with possibility, embodied in Jack Whiteside Parsons, founder of the Jet Propulsion Lab in California, herald of the space age, appointed by Crowley to head the Agape Lodge of the OTO in California in 1942.

Jack Parsons, handsome hip Californian Silver Surfer rocket scientist at Caltech and the Jet Propulsion Lab, taking us all to Jupiter in his shining UFO by way of the otherworld, a Marvel Comics alter-ego, ritual propellant protege of the grand magician, Crowley, Churchill's Dr. Dee, and Parsons waylaid by his very own Ed Kelley in the form of the nemesis L. Ron with their doomed boat business and conjured squalls, Parsons unable to work accused of espionage by McCarthy, Parsons blown to atoms 10 years after Crowley's death by something like fulminate of mercury, the alchemists accelerator, leaving the way clear

**world).
The subverted memory: considering memory as from now-to-now-to-now (In order to remove the accretions of predetermination and expectation as accorded by memory to the possibilities of the future)**

WITH IT'S APPS AND INNOVATIONS AND DIGITAL THINGS AND INTEGRATED THINGS AND DESIGN THINGS AND THE MONEY AND IDEAS AND CONCEPTS AND THIS AND THAT.

Memory as soft and hard: soft=brain, hard=devices

for the cobbled ecstatically prolific Crowleian science fictive therapies of Hubbard, hybrid workings destined to conjure bountiful rewards unto the millennium and beyond with their conflation of science and religion: from the late victorian oriental gothic to the atomic age to the 21st century crystalline consequences of Moore's Law and interstellar overdrive—

(meanwhile in 1958 the artist and designer Gerald Holtom in Britain, working for nuclear disarmament, made a symbol for a march from Trafalgar Square, that symbol of Empire and Victory, to the Atomic Weapons Research establishment in Aldermaston, a symbol for CND using semaphore and allusion to Goya's firing squad—the line, the inverted V, the circle, all ritual and despair and the death of man and the unborn child—a magical working if ever there was, later discreditors of the peace movement claiming similarities to witches' runes and swastikas: as if that would seem discrediting to the movement given those symbols' deeply human and compassionate original provenance)—

**In-between,
or overlap, or
aggregate—
memory
(soft-hard),
memory(soft/
hard),
memory
(soft+hard)**

IT ALL OUGHT TO BE SO MUCH SIMPLER.

Softmemory: remembering, nostalgia, elegy, reminisce, experience, understanding, coincidence, consideration, reflection, recognising, confusion, reverie, dream, ritual, will, now, future (and on), decision

—so Gerald Gardner visits Robert Graves in Majorca colliding and conjuring from ancient groves an Aquarian Age and the rituals become happenings, happening every day: Parks took her rightful place, Pagans flourish, Crowley joins the Lonely Hearts Club Band, the Age is Dawning everywhere as the children of the children of the theosophists return to the east and flourish the magickal V sign, a sign of peace, and the children of the new world fly to the moon, the one following Crowley's map, the other propelled by Parson's fuel, everyone all together now there's nothing you can't do ("what thou wilt") and as Leary was love so Manson was madness and one thing to another and then Altamont and Nixon and there's nothing you can do except regroup in rougher domains and speak stronger wards to the ever-encroaching darkness.

Some things shifting: when Coretta Scott King took leadership of the civil rights movement the remit broadened, driven by the swelling 2nd wave of feminism, into women's rights, and barriers and Stonewalls in the mind and in the world began to

Triggers, shocks, galvanises, conceives, judges (includes to leave well alone)

THE EXECUTIVE SIGHS.

Hardmemory: action, recording, processing, manipulating, building, overlaying, texturing, transforming, power, manifesting

crumble, but too slowly . . .

As the century entered autumn, and the song remained the sigil, and the sigil became the swastika again, both as cathartic iconoclasm (McLaren & Westwood magickal provocateurs when we needed them most) and cruel bigotry (the NF), a woman in New York surrounds Johnny with horses and a young man in Macclesfield is writing songs that told the story of love and death, magic and science, of desolation and rebirth: songs that have the cast of prophetic scrying under the shadow of the mushroom cloud, rich in a formal, ritual language sung to an image of a dying star: and even as he took his own life the light that flourished still shines undimmed: as the swastika reverted and became a New Gold Dream, housed in an ecstatic Hacienda of infinite possibilities, the Bushwhackers embracing at sunrise under the fluffiest of clouds—for the briefest of fleeting moments we weren't fighting, we were feeling, an energy as ephemeral as starlight, fuelled with the last embers of anger and the first inklings of the exponential, a bite from another Apple that folded time and offered infinite

Acts, makes, builds, produces (without predetermination or expectation)

We are enrapt in your spheres: they descend to imprison us, filled with dark ichor, deep ruddy, emerald, copper against an earth-grey sky. The worm has burrowed under the hill.

Long before it all seemed stolen—in so many ways—from me, I'd play and wander the old sewage farm, the land between the bungalows and the dunes, the undeveloped fields and copses of the suburban drift, blending from unfenced back garden to wide open free space, bisected by the straight 60mph roads, before speed bumps, dots of past-

SO NOW, THE LOVELY LUNCH ARRIVES.

seeing-as (entering)— inside starting— the moment— perception— when things change forever— it is not possible to see as before— awakening— immediate complete conception in the conscious— the infinite possible;

possibility, filtering all media and messages together in criss-cross rhythms exploding with happiness . . .

sound & vision and sharks & sheep and tents and champagne supernovae across the heavens: everyone 'avin it large 'avin it major all outward and puffed up and spaced, proud and after 18 years of unrelenting bleak control and constraint and money worship the cycle began again under the guise of the new, the liberating, the tolerant: for a time the parties and pavilions and think-tanks and initiatives seemed convincing, rosy red. Everyone was invited under the dome and gradually the realisation grew that there was nothing in there, a vacuum of empty space where something should be—a thought, a plan, an inspiration, a spirit, a word, a moment, a whisper—anything at all—anything—something—anything at all . . .

another ten years in sound & fury, triggered by horror: a terrible twin collapsing and war everywhere, a war against terror: now we wage war on concepts, the elephant in the room, the unbalanced masculine allowing

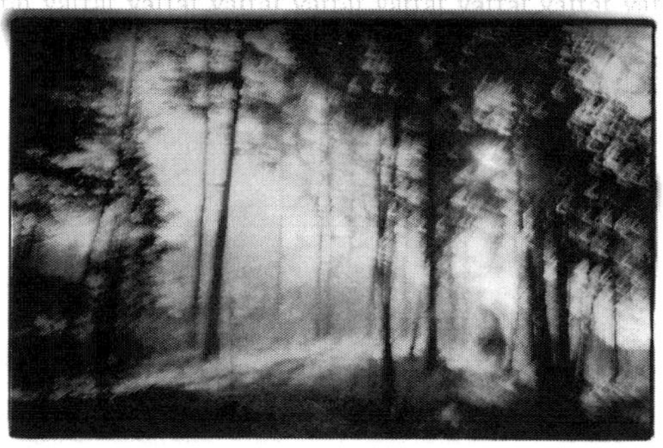

Heroic hours rain grey
at first, then a gate and then
fading, to end
miles out on ghost tracks peter away

Into the trees.
running & running.
and he hears the song.
strange & deep.
rumbling in the earth,
in the trunks of the trees,
in the clouds, in his blood.

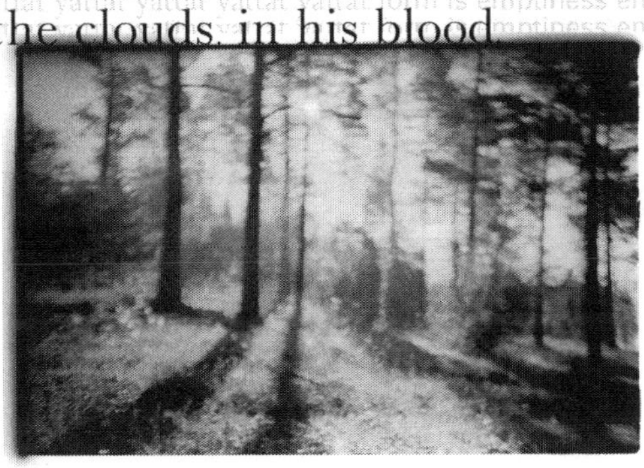

context (questions)— strategies and pathways— mapping— visiting similar places and things— precedent— tradition;

urban pre-country that
we spent our days and
dusks exploring, trying
and not quite succeeding
to get lost forever.
With friends, running
and hiding, cycling;
away from enemies,
escaping, hiding; ever
so slight danger seeming
insurmountable peril;
the huge buried concrete
tunnels behind the school

THE LUNCH IS LIGHT.

dynamic (physicality) agitating— making— sculpting— moving— the thing— outside;

murder, unleashing the worst on the worst with no sense of reason except that of the moment: twisting the beautiful poetics and legends and grand mythologies of human imagination into the cruel absolutes of religion, a sinister front for atrocity and abuse from birth to death . . . all a generation could do is reach into the past to create the most tenuous now with no map or waypost or food or fuel, nothing but what had gone before recycled beyond all use, reused, drinking our own piss, squeezed to the very last retro ironic drop. The destination was everything: the dry well, the karaoke stage, X marks the spot, X for the treasure, X the known, X the negated, X nothing, X a whimpering 'NO' to thought or possibility or chance or beauty: X, the nothing factor, the dead point overseen by a ghoul cowled in shadow leeching all light and colour from the possible future . . .

Bamber, Carrington, Castle, Deren, Goodall, Grenfell, Hepworth, Hodgkin, Kahlo, Mead, Murdoch, Pankhurst, Parks, Rodoreda, Smith, Springfield, Stopes, Szabo, Westwood, Woolf, Yousafzai . . .

. . . but now there's

obstacle
(conflict) —
the finite
possible —
blockage —
restriction —
reworking —
adverse — ;

claimed as pre-world war hideouts. Beside the railway station and the scrap yard, the empty car park with our scrap ramps, nail-punctured tyres, riding two to a bike what seemed until the ends of our earth.

These were the landscapes of our summers, echoing with imagination and invention and tattle.

AND JUST FOR THE EXQUISITE MOMENT THE EXECUTIVE IS FINE.

negotiation (adjustment)— shift— remodel— compromise— judgement—;

inklings: far from the nonsense farrago of a twisted polis sedated and conditioned by the words whispering from the papers and the telly there are sounds and images feeling like brighter things: George Ives' struggle germinating in union, a new generation finding their own way through the lights and lights in space and time rising apart and separate streaming, joining in the flow, the true main stream of the dreaming adventurers, together, growing, not self-absorbed, growing up and away from the impulse to 'just do it', to 'do what thou wilt', growing together with no borders between them, no cruelty or judgement, no grudges or assumptions and presumptions, no waiting idly, meekly, desperately for permission: considerate, passionate, awake, compassionate, travelling deep in history, out in the world, living for love where the feminine holds sway, where the muse is adored as the moon far away in the orient, sister of the mirage and the echo, and where the Swastika was born in the Indus Valley, a sign for well-being and auspiciousness among Hindus and Buddhists alike for thousands of years, stolen by a

still (removal from the process)— emptiness— no-mind— rest—;

The man with the white gloves and the sunglasses who lived near the railway, leaning over his balcony most days, who had a collection of horror films (in those days they would have been super 8 or 16mm celluloid). The hill in the middle of the sewage farm (actually a rough grassland with criss-crossing tracks running through it) that we could never quite find a way to surmount. Climbing through the tree tops like monkeys.

The First Commandment: Know Thy Customer

response (the thing in the world)— an object— apart— intrinsic— leaving— outside;

madman, painted on a forehead, a doorway, among the stars, and perhaps to be reclaimed deep inside the mind, a recasting from symbols ancient and modern now new together as one, a golden intersection, one thing containing everything that can mean something new again, a new sign for humanity, a 'no sign', no mind, unconditioned, gnothi seauton, a sign for constant change, dreaming its own dreams and building anew again together through experience and understanding with imagination above all to create together, gods & goddesses alike, surrendering and seeking, to make change together publicly and loudly in the streets and through the unfettered strands of the web in joyful revolution, children learning, observing the golden rule above all in balance with the sun and the moon as we face with love the stark and revealing tabula rasa of our selves and our future: our collective responsibility for what has gone before, and to live up to what is to come.

*Bike punctures. Sprains.
Stitch from running.
But above all, the holes
in fences, deep puddles,
concrete blocks, thistles
and nettles, white dog
shit, bright sunlight,
rusting corrugated iron,
and all the skids, trips,
blows, skills and scabs
that mean nothing to no
one except me alone.*

*Specific places, at specific
times, with specific
names—Harvington,
Clock House Station,
Elmers End sewage
farm—discovered by me
and my friends and no
one else, places few in
number, that no longer
exist because we are not
there, and would not
be there now, even if I
visited because I am not
what I was; they were
beautiful and they are
gone, red admiral and
peacock and cabbage
white, lost to geography
and time, and they
are not inspiration,
or part of a process, or
revived through that
form of documentary-
without-a-subject, fiction*

Method
Process
Systems
Process
Method

Rituals marking out time and space: called by dreams (? Waking- and sleeping-)

And Sublimations
we make for three
causes,
The first cause is
to make the body
spiritual.
The second is that
the spirit may be
corporeal,
And become
fixed with it and
consubstantial.
The third cause is
that from its filthy
original
It may be cleansed,
and its saltiness
sulphurious
May be diminished
in it, which is
infectious.
George Ripley
(Alchemist, ca 1415-1490)

i remember it clearly: a drawing class on foundation course. previously we had been introduced to grids. the greyscale. hand rendering. the drawing class was a little looser, to do with landscape. one class had us drawing layers of soil, undergrowth. this time, the tutor asked us to look at the window, at the view outside, at the room surrounding the window, but to imagine what we were seeing as flat, not dimensional.
this changed the way i saw the world.

from one moment to the next, i went from being an observer of the things around—

imagination known as 'psychogeography'; I cannot go back, and they would mean nothing if

I could show you, and they are nothing that can be taken away and reclaimed, because they only existed for me and my friends when we were young.

IT IS A NICE FINE DAY.

Entering spaces and times—initiation, crossing over

to seeing. suddenly i could see the interrelationship of things. lines intersecting. shapes overlapping, interrupting. shapes and shade. structure, pattern, form. the drama of form. in the world. in myself. no longer just outside. everywhere. the expressive world. tension. drift. emotion. light.

Symbols
Stone
circles
Mandala
Sand
mandala

i remember other moments.

i remember a 12 inch record label, the label for Pearly Dewdrops Drops by The Cocteau Twins. it felt like my glimpse was slipping; like i couldn't see it because i didn't know what it was. i didn't know how to see it.

i felt like i had been handed the means with which i could always make something: beyond 'inspiration', this was innate. it had become part of me. more, even, than reflex. as if some exchange had taken place. a change of state. because one person suggested i look out a window.

One of the main stages of the alchemical magnum opus is the "transmutation of silver into gold", called Citrinitas (yellowness).

The process by which a substance transitions from solid to gas without passing through the liquid stage is known as Sublimation.

Sublimation is used by chemists to purify compounds. Citrinitas (xanthosis) is

BUT OH.

Movement/ shaman; altered state, ecstasy— entering

Numbers — sacred geometry, Vitruvian man. Fibonacci. Octaves. Harmonics. Circles/ alchemy/ magick: gestures and tools, drawing in air, with fire, on earth. Seven elements.

OH NO.

the light by which understanding is illuminated.

Below zero, snow and ice sublime.

In alchemy, Sublimation is the process by which body becomes spirit, and vice versa.

George Ripley's alchemical 12 Gates are:
1. Calcination
2. Solution (or Dissolution)
3. Separation
4. Conjunction
5. Putrefaction
6. Congelation
7. Cibation
8. Sublimation
9. Fermentation
10. Exaltation
11. Multiplication
12. Projection

A working process.

Like any other.

Colours

Musical notation, working to music, drawing music as it is heard

1

eyes, watery, blue, infinite and forever—and he blinks, so slowly, closed for a moment too long—the pale skin marked with small sunbursts, red, aching, broken—while his clothes, all black, hang like dying leaves—they are too worn to welcome strangers, too stained—and he reaches out his hand, his long grey hand—while his mouth framed with thin young hair moves in speech—and he keeps on—over and over—his silver crutches tucked under his arms—so simple—he asks—please help me—he asks of the people stopped in their cars—over and over—leaning into their windows, their worlds—only ever just asking—between the cars—at the junction where they all have to stop—on the pavement, on the tarmac—still going—waiting for his world to change—holding on so his world can stay the same—a symbol of what life just leaves behind, waiting—unknown to the past and unaware of what will come—not speaking please help me but asking for a coin—to buy the sun—to buy the sky—again—again—again—again—slowly—again—a drift—again—a coin to buy a name—some time—please help me—again

2

a face, eyes closed, finger to lips, 'shhh'. a man in his garden, pottering. the garden is large: it is obviously a back garden. the man notices his fence begin to shake. he steps for a moment, staring. the fence moves again as if someone has hold of it and is shaking it for all they are worth. it happens once more, harder and faster, and the man, worried, steps up to the fence to investigate. he peers over it, looking right, looking left, and seeing nothing. it shakes again while he is peering, and to the far right, at the corner, he can see a hand clutching and shaking the fence. carefully, quietly, he approaches the corner, dragging his rake. the shaking stops again, and everything is still. the man crouches behind the fence, waiting: then he darts up, rake poised, looking over. there is another man there, crouching by the fence corner. he gives a strange, twisted leer, holds his fingers to his lips 'shhh', and darts off over the hill, towards the tree. the man stands, stunned. he drops his rake. he takes half a step forward, stops, takes another little step: by now, the 'shhh' man is behind the tree. the tree starts to shake, really violently, as if something far bigger than the little man is doing it. the man jumps over his fence, and starts to walk towards the tree. a face peeks out from behind, and makes his 'shhh'. he scampers off towards the trees. the man follows, running now, moving faster down the hill towards the forest. the little man leaps through the trees, taking longer and wider steps, looking back over his shoulder. as he does, his eyes light up green and green and red, shifting colour as he smiles and grins. the garden man still follows, his steps growing wider and wider, too, and soon the little mans steps are out of all proportion to his size: he is bounding through the forest, arms pumping, eyes blazing, taking off.

COLOURED PAPER NAPKINS.

Grids—

3 BIGGEST RESUME MISTAKES

bauhaus/ swiss

SOMETHING!

yes there is something yes i can see it
i can know it is within and without
it is my experience it is my understanding
it is tangible it makes me feel

Sigils—Austin Osman Spare: language/method/as form

NO.

5ft. 10ft strides that launch him 10, 15, 20 feet in the air. as he does so, his arms and legs seem to grow, lengthening impossibly as he moves. the gardener starts to catch him up, and he is propelled higher and higher by their great strides. now, their leapy, boundy running takes them up to the treetops. shining, twinkling, they run on and on, the leaves their pathway. now, they are running, leaping and soaring across the treetops, up into the sky, and they leave trails of green and gold and red behind them, filled with joy, laughing and leaping, higher and higher until till they run on and on, the leaves their pathway. now, they are running, leaping and soaring across the treetops, up into the sky, and they leave trails of green and gold and red behind them, filled with joy, laughing and leaping, higher and higher until they are passing the stars in the twilight sky and all of a sudden they both pop out of existence with an aurora flash over the trees, the colour folding back on itself into two bright new stars, shining, twinkling. one of the stars fades out of existence, and in the other you can just see a face, winking and holding its finger to its lips, 'shhh'. in the mans garden, over his cabbage patch, a little aurora shines out, and the man pops out of it, falling back to earth. he opens his eyes and they twinkle, green and gold and red.

3

we see a large room-low light, looks like there are curtains filling one end of the room. the camera travels towards them as the light grows. the curtains, deep, night blue in colour, with tiny mirrors sewn into them reflecting the light like stars, start to draw apart. slowly, they reveal a silhouette, a figure of a man in a cloak, backlit with those deep oranges of an early dawn, standing on an empty stage. he starts to raise his arms to the air, and the light, slowly, very slowly; he wears a cloak; it is made from the same material as the curtain, except it is blood-red instead of blue. the figure moves, expressively, but staying in his place in the centre of the stage, and soon is joined by two more figures, dressed in sunburst leotards, one from each side of the stage. the two figures dance around the man, and soon they are joined by two more, their costumes a slightly different shade of sunburst, brighter in colour. the light starts to get stronger, the mans cloak reflects the light, echoing the changing brightness around him. we start to see now: behind them, at the back of the stage, gradually revealed by the growing light, shapes and forms like the rays of the sun. another figure joins the man on stage, but this time it is a woman dressed in a cloak like the mans, except hers is vibrant golden yellow. she approaches him, and they dance close and hard, wilder the others, their long hair entwining as they lose themselves in each other. another pair of dancers enters stage, two more figures, dressed in sunburst flared leotards, one from each side of the stage. the light gets brighter still, revealing more fully the graphic shapes of the sunrise at the back of the stage; the shapes move, shifting up and down, pulsing like

Iconotropy— Robert Graves and The White Goddess

PHENOMENA!

so many things i don't know and never will
people and places and things and senses
wind gravity magnetism electricity fields
not to touch to know to feel enough infinite
one life not enough/more than enough

Use of computers as modern ritual/ html css

the dawn, and two more dancers join the couple on stage in their wild ritual, and another pair, and another pair, and now there is a circle of dancers moving in unison, now splitting apart, dressed in the graduated colours of the sunrise as an enormous silver globe descends from above them, its surface rippling like oil, reflecting on all of them, and the man and the woman drop their cloaks and are dressed in silver and gold, and the light now is vivid and filled with the sun as the dancers lift them above their heads and glitter and bubbles and tinsel falls all over them, and a banner unfurls over the stage with the word 'unicorn' on it in old english text, colour graduating from deep orange to bright yellow on a white background, as the silhouette of a huge motorbike rearing its head rises behind them, the spokes of it's wheels backlit by the light of the fake sunrise.

+
planets

a lake, a house, some trees, a cardboard box seems to move by itself down towards the lake shore, it stops, flips over, and a child, a boy, aged about 7 or 8 stands up from under the box and walks towards an apparently dead tree, carrying a metal bucket. he puts the bucket on the ground by the tree and stands, stretching. the environment is cold, but not barren — beautiful, there is the sky, rocks, trees, grassy fields, a lake; and a big house. the child crouches and arranges some stones around a dead tree branch, the stone's weight holding the branch upright, like a small dead tree. he picks up the bucket and pours water onto the stones, watering the tree. he walks back, towards the house, it is getting dark; his father is calling him inside.

nightime. inside the house, the boy's father studies astronomical drawings, charts, old manuscripts detailing the phases of the planets. he sets up a small computerised telescope by a window, near a lotus flower, butterflies under glass, an aquarium containing silkworms, programming co-ordinates. he puts his eye to the eye piece. the stars reflect in his pupil. they seem to make a pattern there. something is growing, changing. the father goes to the bathroom, looking in the mirror, he removes his contact lenses.

next day, morning, the child comes out of the house, walking to the tree, carrying his bucket. he stops and waters the tree again, stepping back and looking up at the branches. they are bare. he goes back to the house. his father is outside, staring at the sky. the child touches his fathers leg and goes inside. the father walks out to the fields, losing himself in the waves of the tall grasses. he comes to a rise, looking out to the next hill. he looks at the contrails of airplanes in the sky.

night. the father starts looking in his telescope, the millions of stars shift, move in tiny waves, until he focuses on one, a small point of light that seems to be unfolding. his eyes reflect the luminosity of the aurora borealis, heading overhead, descending towards the house, the stunning ribbons of electric energy reach closer to the ground, covering the house

THE EXECUTIVE'S HEART FEELS BROKEN.

Time & space boundaries; marking out areas ; timing and budget = ritual

CONTROL!

with consideration and balance in all moments
from moment to moment emotion ready to flow
to extremes with care with thought and foresight
grateful for life and living utmost where living will take me
and now at this point of divergence all things are possible
all things to be discovered all things to be explored
from within to without control the realisation the control is death

Setting/ preparing state of mind in order to enter the memory to disturb things into being

and passing through its rooms. the child goes out into the night. looking straight up into the sky. next morning, the child goes out to the tree, carrying his bucket. he stops, looking back to his father at the house, who stands, looking at the tree. the child approaches the apparently dead branch, held up by the stones, and sees one small bud, just starting to open, in the branches of the tree.

5

a man is walking through a park with a thin blue plastic bag. the ground beneath his feet gets soggier and muddier, and he takes off his shoes and squelches through the mud.

it gets more like a bog, beyond his ankles, so he takes his trousers off to keep them clean. somehow, though, he loses his bag, the thin blue plastic sinking out of reach beneath the mud. he reaches a high street and heads towards a bar.

he goes to the bar and it's huge, a sandy-coloured room with only about a dozen people. they all stare at him, and he realises that he's got no shoes or trousers on, and mud stains his legs up to the knees. the bar has a water feature, very realistic, a big pond with reeds and rocks as stepping stones across. he hops from rock to rock, but halfway along he slips on the wet stone and plunges into the water. underwater, there is a cave entrance, another bar. he swims towards it.

6

a huge fat man, dressed very smartly, walks into a supermarket, rushing to a trolley in a blur of nervous energy. everyone in the supermarket is standing still, uncomfortably, some of them moving a bit, some smiling to themselves, and some of them stare at him and frown. he doesn't notice at first, but then slowly he realises and becomes embarrassed, uncomfortable. suddenly he is bright red, embarrassed—he is naked, and pale green sweat pours off him in rivulets, collecting on the floor. the sweat pours so fast that soon it is up to everyones ankles, and they become agitated, darting looks at each other, licking their lips and beginning to grin. one young man can't contain himself any longer, and drops to his knees in slow motion, the beautiful green liquid sparkling like crystal and splashing around him, catching the light like liquid diamonds, and he cups his hands and dips them in the liquid and drinks, drinking deeply. the big red man beams a smile, and turns an emerald green colour, the light filling the supermarket as he rises from the floor and disappears in whirling green-golden light.

A breeze stirs dust motes awake, glittering in moonlight

THE 5 TRAITS OF THE AGENCY OF THE FUTURE

UNCANNY!
to look directly into darkness
to walk upright under the moon
to embrace horror
live pain
to understand the true meaning of balance
taboo indulgence transgression transcendence
to realise the equanimity of all things
to know all parts as the whole

AUTO-D

NO

THEY WRITHE
WRACK
JUSTIFY
THEIR WRETC
TWISTING IN
A CRUEL POS
SPINNING
ABSURD MAJ

THE

TO FUEL THE

REVULS

RTAUG

ESTRUCT!

W!

ED STANDING
ACE
ION

STY
IES
SHITTY ENGINES
ION

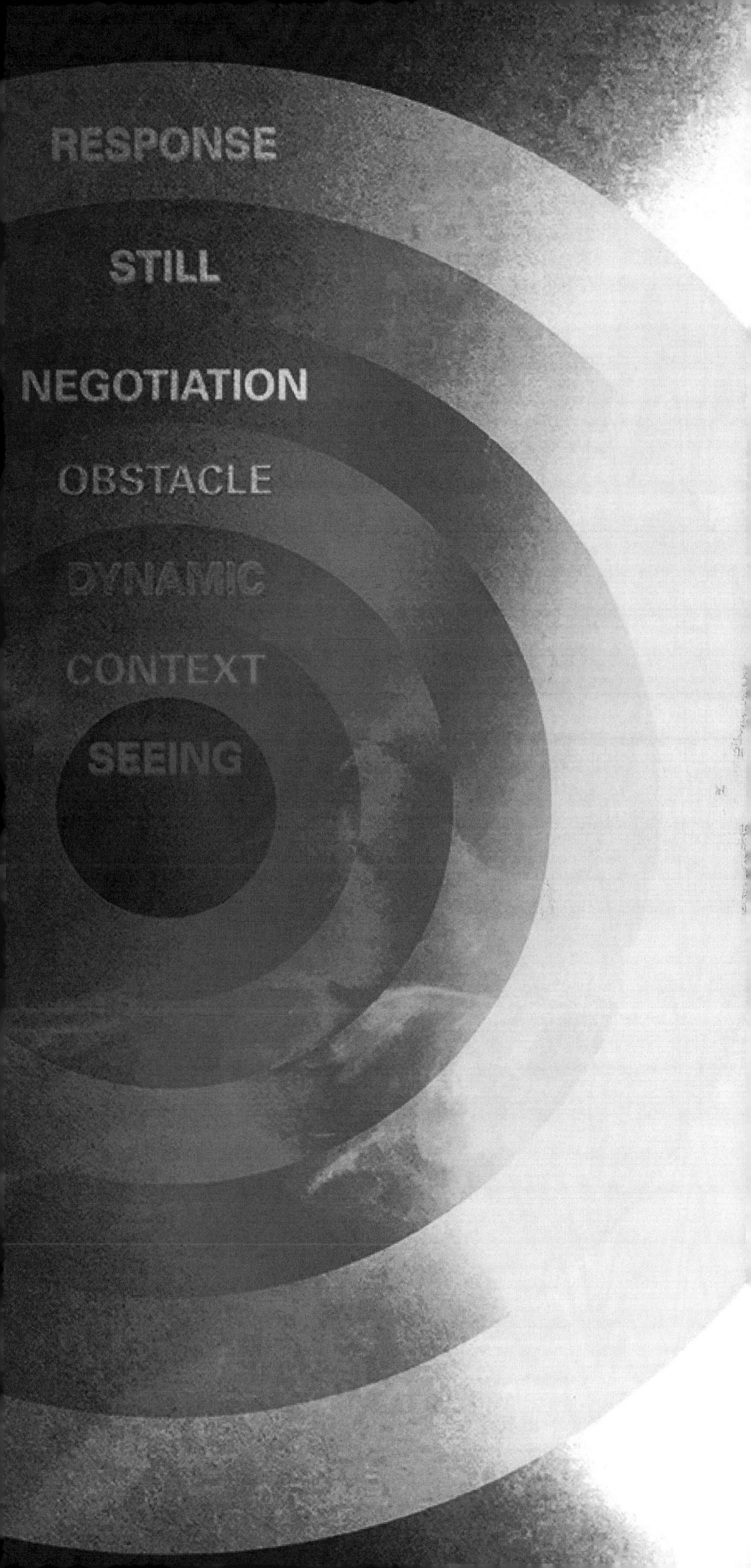
RESPONSE
STILL
NEGOTIATION
OBSTACLE
DYNAMIC
CONTEXT
SEEING

childhood seems so far away; and yet still i'm here, inside, from one moment to the next all as it was. i ask, "what moves? do i travel or does the world pass by?" of course, i leave my home, one foot in front of the other, get on a train, or a plane; and so on. but equally i could say that there is something, that seems to be 'me', that is within, or possibly even elsewhere, that remains in a still state as, outside, everything moves in swooping curves, intersecting lines; great sheets of colour, temperature, sound . . . time, and space, move on around, swirling; childhood seems so far away; i am a child.

an elegy is (among other things) "a song or poem expressing sorrow or lamentation especially for one who is dead", and "a pensive or reflective poem that is usually nostalgic or melancholy". Jacques Brel's song, "Mon Enfance", while on first impression seemingly a cry for lost dreams, an observation on the descent into lassitude and the bourgeois that comes with middle-age, (surely elegiac), is, to me, a song about the death of childhood, both in individual and societal ("Et la guerre arriva") terms. The sure, unjust murder of love (in its childhood sense) through the wasting of the apparently illusory powers of the imagination (definitely elegiac). there never was a Far West.

the notion of "The Far West"- an Eden, a Never-never land, an eternal, unchanging place of childhood and love and peace and plenty, an invention revealed as a panacea, a fatal loss-while deeply elegiac; melancholy; is something that is perhaps a way of understanding this feeling of internal foreverness, serenity. the simultaneous loss of and continual state of childhood, or adolescence—every age and thing that you've ever experienced, all at once, gone.

3) Even a stopped clock . . .

5 TIPS FOR MARKETING ONLINE TO AN INTERNATIONAL AUDIENCE

—What if, as a user, i want to return to my ‘digital’ experience in 20 years’ time? (I’ve got some cd-roms here . . .)

—Trinkets, baubles, shadowplay, fol-de-rol, misdirection, trickery, pablum, puffery, sham, veneer, schtick, artifice, display, guise, subterfuge, facade, ruse, guise, charade; the ways and means of the so-called 'content' vacuum packed by the 'experience'

—If a thing wants to become a 'field', a 'discipline', an art or a science, it makes for a better case if the application of the thing doesn't tend to produce similar, anonymous results

—Your remit is not homogeneity but variety

5 WEIRD HABITS THAT MAKE PEOPLE SUCCESSFUL AND AWESOME

PERCEPTION!
my senses and my mind are not enough
i am only human
but i am a star
among the countless number
i am i
in the universe
the universe is not i
but
i the universe!

—Set up circumstances where copying is just not possible

—It is said that repeating the same thing over and over again in expectation of differing results is clearly insanity

—You can't have your cake and eat it; you're either contributing to a project in an inspiring way or you're not involved. Taking credit for the best bits; or ducking responsibility for the ill-conceived; you're a charlatan.

SYNTHESIS!
Unity!

"The joy of life consists in the exercise of one's energies, continual growth, constant change, the enjoyment of every new experience. To stop means simply to die. The eternal mistake of mankind is to set up an attainable ideal."
Aleister Crowley

—You’re nothing without something.

—It is about the thing, not the thing itself. To confuse one for the other is dangerous. The experience is not the thing.

—The notion about memory.

THE EXECUTIVE CRIES FOR ALL THAT HAS BEEN LOST.

reeform, play and so on. a state of mind, time of day and on and on . . .

see them.
see.

ffects of the 'fixed' object. It is pure
ost powerful thing in life. It is life.

istributed, an audience experiences it and
function in this way (think about gossip,
cles, call and response, inspiration,

iewpoints-macro and micro.

and a long term working process, there is
must go on, I can't go on, I'll go
another, then another, and so on. This is
influence not only on the quality and
at, rather than a kind of melange of
s possible and possibly wonderful), the
o maintain a sense of openness and
can be a bit diminishing. Here, there is a
nge? Which become entrenched? What
effect on the kinds of things produced
late something that is a feeling to me, like
ally overwhelming . . . the psychological
eived, where it takes you . . . everything
dview is from that perspective-this is

the form of the loop is a seductive and
pes, textures, patterns and so with
thinking, the looping process can lead into
d as practical as laying out a large amount

behavior that causes events to galvanise the physical and emo
process at every point, from conception to memory, experien

The 'loop' is a prevalent theme (concept, tool, objective) in m
responds, the originator in turn responds with another concep
or even more isolated neuroses . . . the closed, internal loop)
influence . . . call it what you will, the loop is a construct that

So with these conceptual terms, how do we explore the aes

In the macro sense, and if we can allow the notion of 'aesthe
one sense in which the loop looms large. This is in the proces
on."-which can allude to the sheer joy/enormity of how one m
the looping effort of a working life, and in the broad sense of
qualities of work, but also on the ability and desire to do it in t
seemingly chaotic, energising and joyful experiences (when th
actuality is of doing it (whatever 'it' is) again and again and ag
awareness and allowing oneself to be inspired and all of that
loop of rhythm and pattern in its largest sense-as one grows c
are discovered to be irrelevant, immature, or damaging? Over
the reasons for doing them. This is somewhat woolly I think, I
a weather system . . . how that affects your day and can add
effects of it, the questioning of it (and by 'it' I mean what one
Work has determined my life-I can see that now-and that's th
where I find myself. I work therefore I am. This is my loop. Th

In the micro sense-the aesthetic of the loop is central to both
inspiring thing. Through overlay and repetition new forms can
emerge out of grids, systems, marks and so on, and by contin
unknown territory, which is good. It may sound intense or con
of type on a grid, or as effortless as daydreaming, but the loop
notion of 'right' (aesthetically) is entwined with the macro vie
happing next, and so on. All loops within loops, constantly fee
because its in the moiré that you find what you're looking for
be a glint of something that implies a whole picture, a sugges

Both consciously and unconsciously, influence is like circles o
shifts and changes over time but never disappears. Cause and
this sense, everything becomes 'both/and'; by this I mean tha

loop is
etition
d so

4) U are not X

making things, imaginative things, things that come alive in the world and proliferate, are shared, held, explored, clicked, read, considered, lost, forgotten: things are never really 'started'— they fade in, or reveal

What this is is really a minor digression on some things that go without saying.

Or some things that once went without saying—a simple, natural part of any working process.

Not any more.

THE EXECUTIVE IS PERTURBED.

It's on the verge of becoming a serious barrier to things being made because its being seen as a thing-in-itself, a thing to use to pre-empt, control, limit and determine; fortunately it's a very young thing which can still learn, can still be freed from the tyranny of first principles, but it isn't anything without things in the first place.

Can you guess what it is?

Anything that is a thing needs to be a thing.

That is to say, you can't do something with nothing.

Which means you need something (here, i'm talking about narrative and journey. Could be talking about an image, or a space, or an object, or. . .) to experience.

And once you have something, then you can (if necessary—if the thing itself doesn't already have this as a natural, integral part of itself), make a decent effort of getting people into, around, and engaged with their experience.

First things first.

What is going to be made?

themselves, appearing out of the previous things that have occurred and propelled by what's happening now and now and now. . . things are never really 'started' they emanate, grow . . . if anything,

'k, th

or-eve
influer

So, wi

d micro.

king process, there is
o on, I'll go
er, and so on. This is
n the quality and
of melange of
ly wonderful),
f openness and
hing. Here, the
entrenched? Wh
f things one does
s a feeling to me, like
. the psychological
you . . . everything.
erspective-this is

is a seductive and
ns and meaning
process can lead into
g out a large amount
ntrinsically 'right'
before, what cou
s is interesting b
ompe l'oeil the

res this interplay that
does with ones life. In
ng that seems fresh

In terms of what the thing needs to be, tone (what kind of emotion are we evoking?), scene (when/where/who/what is this?) and breadth (intimate, singular? Expansive, multifold?) are the seeds to nurture.

What will they grow into?

At this point, there ought to be no 'should', 'has to be', no boxes, no titles, no roles, no 'we were told to . . .' or 'we thought . . .'; what's useful are questions, possibilities, moments, textures, a dry seed pod bursting open . . .

there's a flow, not only in terms of direction but also depth: as the flow propels with faster and slower streams, so you're taken through the depths and shallows, and on as time passes and the will brings

IT SEEMS TO THE EXECUTIVE THAT PEOPLE MAKE NEW THINGS JUST TO EXASPERATE THE EXECUTIVE.

This isn't a careful, conservative occupation. Not if the results are going to be vividly alive. It can be subversive, transgressive and ultimately transcendent.

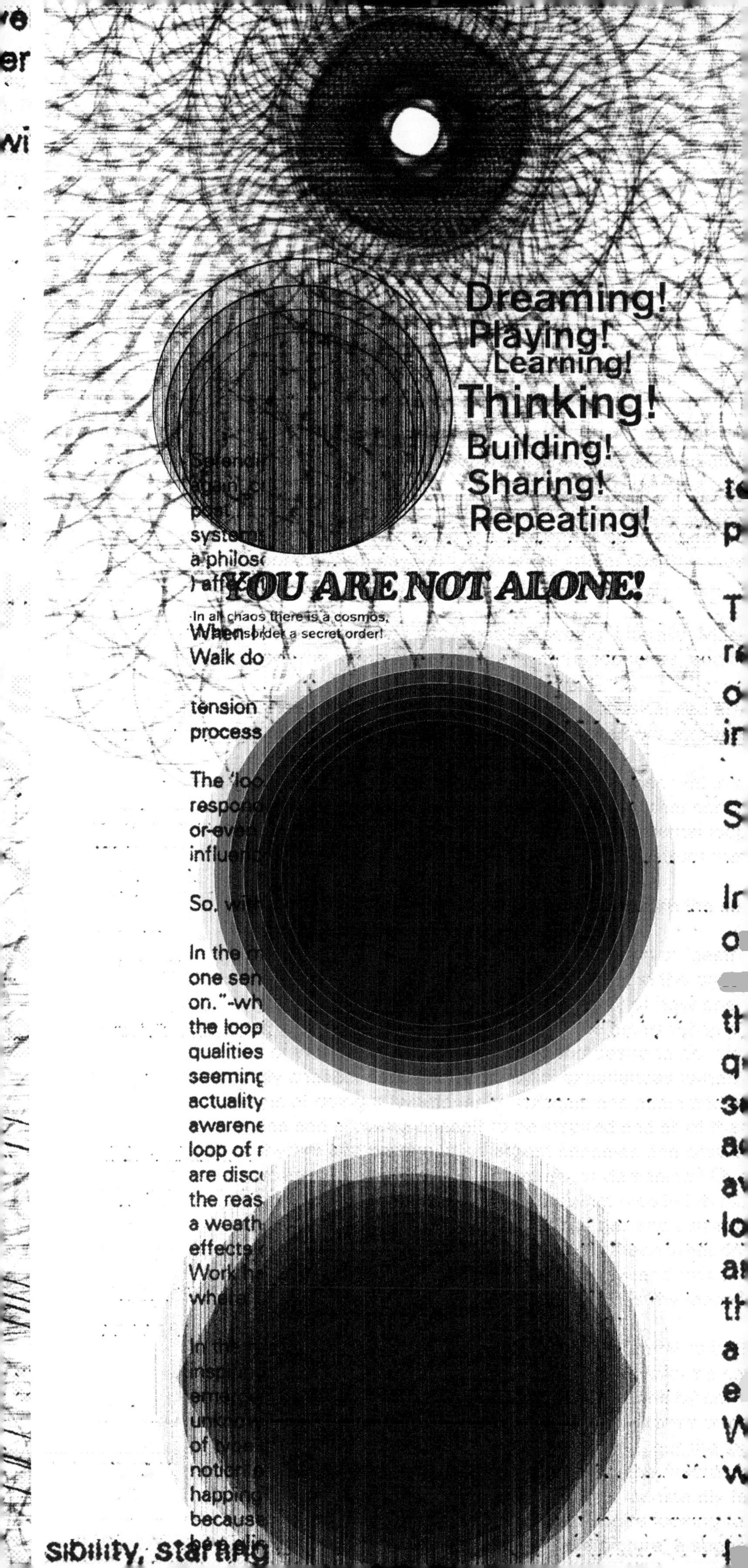
Dreaming!
Playing!
Learning!
Thinking!
Building!
Sharing!
Repeating!
YOU ARE NOT ALONE!
In all chaos there is a cosmos,
in all disorder a secret order!

What are the most enrapturing things you've experienced?

What makes them memorable?

What makes them vivid, or melancholy, or transcendent?

The beauty of creating narratives, journeys, is that digressions can become the thing.

You never know.

Concentration and distraction simultaneous.

Working to structure and build, ready to embrace the unlooked-for, the unexpected—at least, that's the mind state it's worth inhabiting to get things flowing and into some form, becoming some thing. You never know.

Growing—unfolding into an expressive, emotional, living experience.

to life the products of the imagination.

there it is. no more or less simple than that. no ego, justification, competition: a something that feels like an attempt at remembering that manifests as something

IT SEEMS TO THE EXECUTIVE THAT JUST MAINTAINING A SATISFACTORY EVEN KEEL ON COURSE FOR TARGET EQUILIBRIUM ISN'T ENOUGH ANY MORE.

Then, it's possible to begin mapping the journey into, around, and out of the thing as a natural part of reviewing, refining and producing the thing.

Discovery.

Seeing things for what they are.

Seed pods bursting into life.

Not examining the seed pod with a microscope for signs of life because it can't be trusted, in order to control it, but letting it be because you know it will be set free by the process—the whole process.

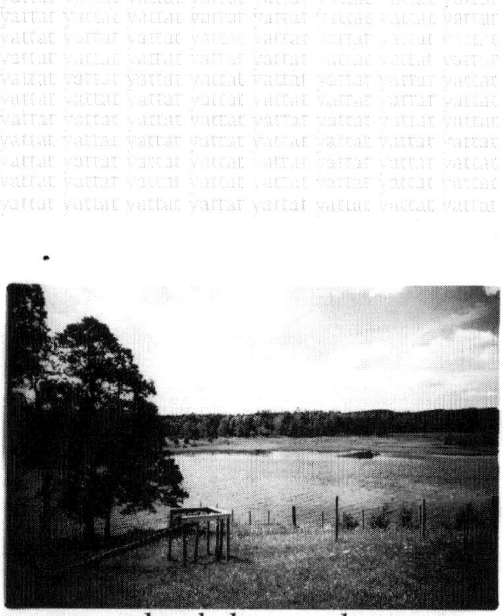

Down to the lake, and over there the cows lowing, flies all around, midges & tiny black flies, sharp pinpricks all over again & again, on the hands & face, red swells flaring.

Memory becomes everything —
least alongside , prone outlaid
tending the quiet time .
Here we are , arranged
the no-action , no-thought
no-decision ,
guilt
sublime beguiled
a point or a stand
each side equal , squared ,
leaving no space by space defined
relative one thing
the source and ending ,
the re-creation , reliving
an existing procession ;
upon the leaves
the contact emerges

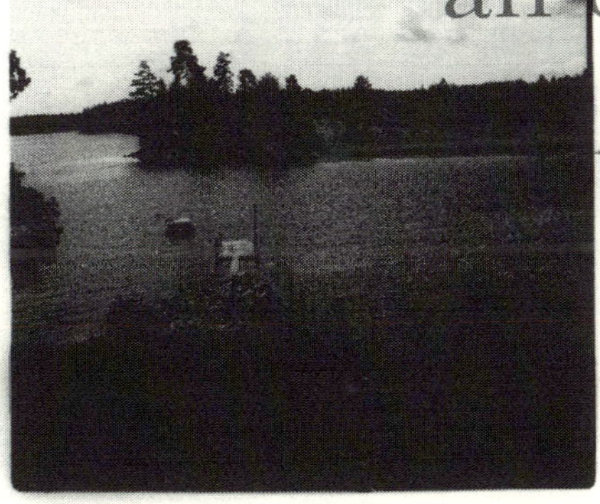

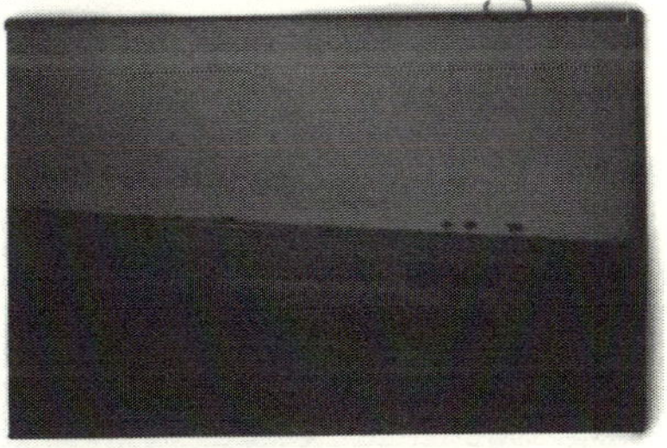

Letting it explode open and seeing what grows. Hopefully, what comes out will be unrecognisable, unjudgeable, polarising, extraordinary.

A thing that i, as a user (whether on a page, on a screen, in a space, in a portfolio . . .), can experience in wonder.

If i want to.

that can be experienced. willing the latent pulse into dormant dreaming. collaborating, time and again. a shared language that becomes almost exclusively gestural. lightness. play,

nd so c
y sour
dream
ed wit
n loop
hat yo
hole p

luenc
dis
nd
f play,
, and s
ncou
k, th

Conjure!
This is the Map!
Your Satellite!
YOU ARE NOT ALONE!
Transformation, healing, initiation,
construction or destruction!

it's al

How

Can I

That

That

That

Sere
agair
post
syste
a phi
aff

Whe
Walk

tensi
proce

The
resp
or-ev
influe

So. v

nd micro.

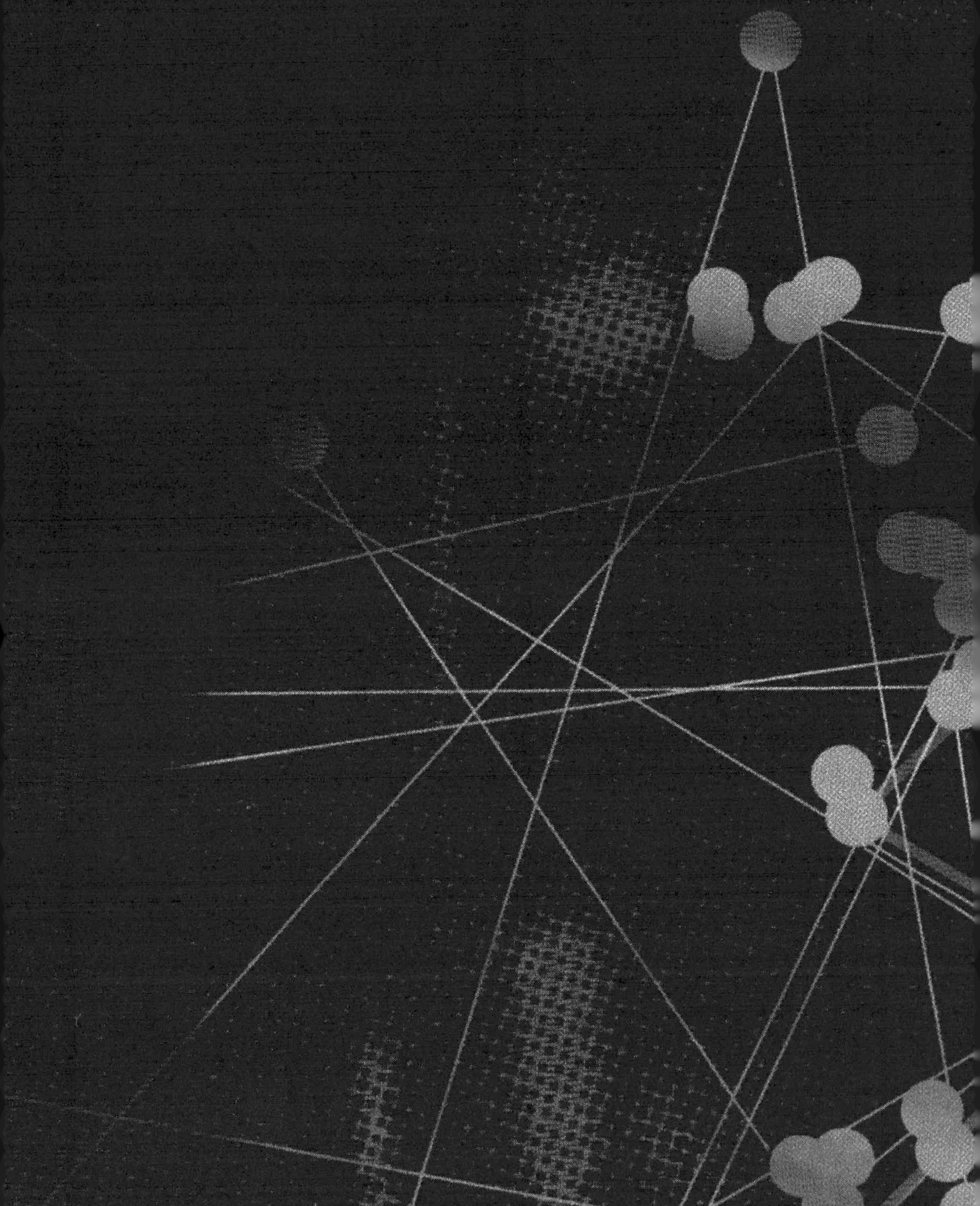

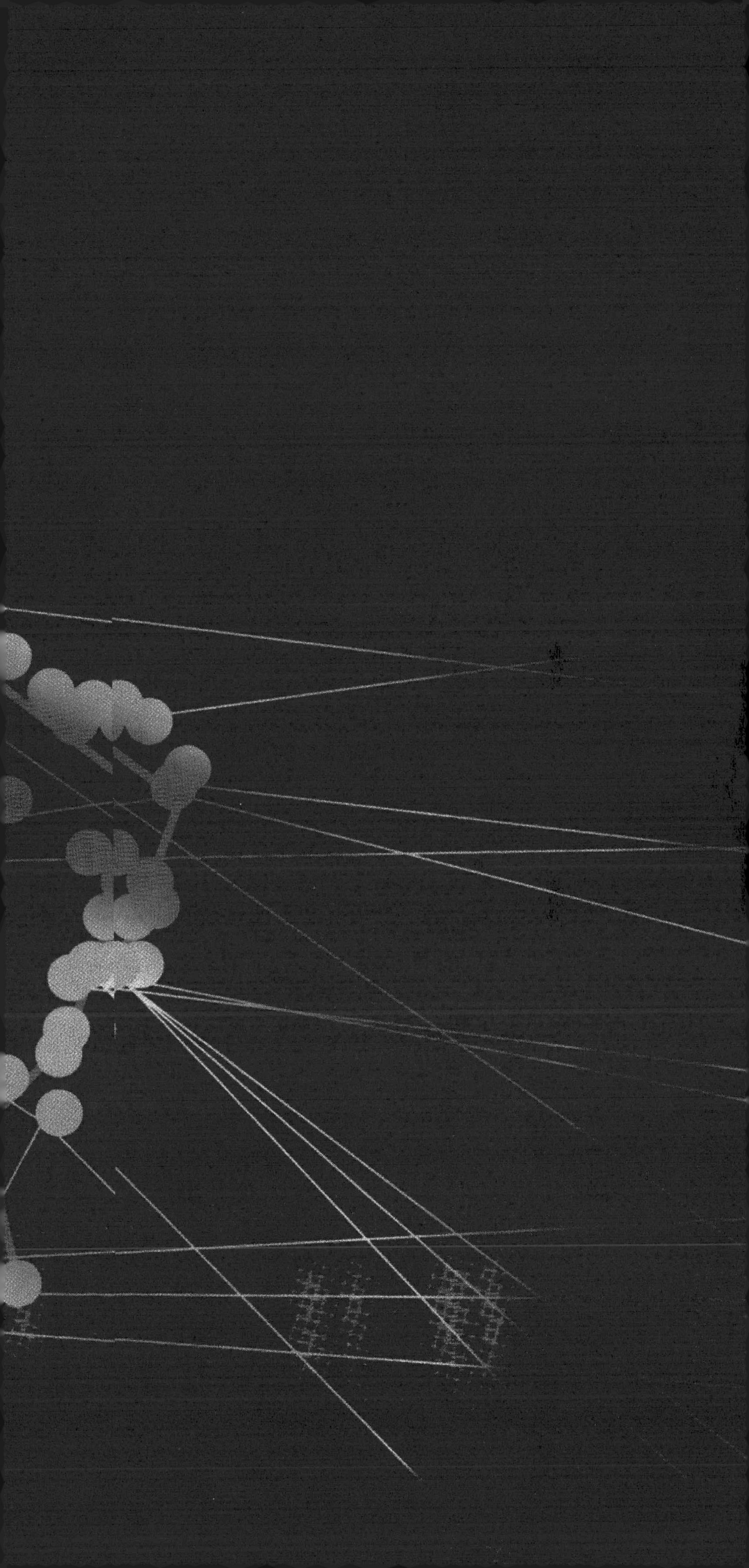

5) This is This

humour, joy. not looking for the one perfect (arch, smug, pained, drained, constrained etc,) thing alone, but making multitudes simultaneously, always, together. because if not

Experience is not the thing itself. Experience is what is caused by the thing; how it is discovered, used, understood, misunderstood and so on (etc).

We have our prior experience of things—we tend to say ‘i’m looking forward to . . .’ Or ‘i’m not looking forward to . . .’

We have our post-experience of things—we tend to say (in short) either 'it was good' or 'it was bad'. Perhaps 'it was ok', which tends to mean better than bad.

with ones life, in
that seems fresh,
g other which can
able, but you
nding, sharing

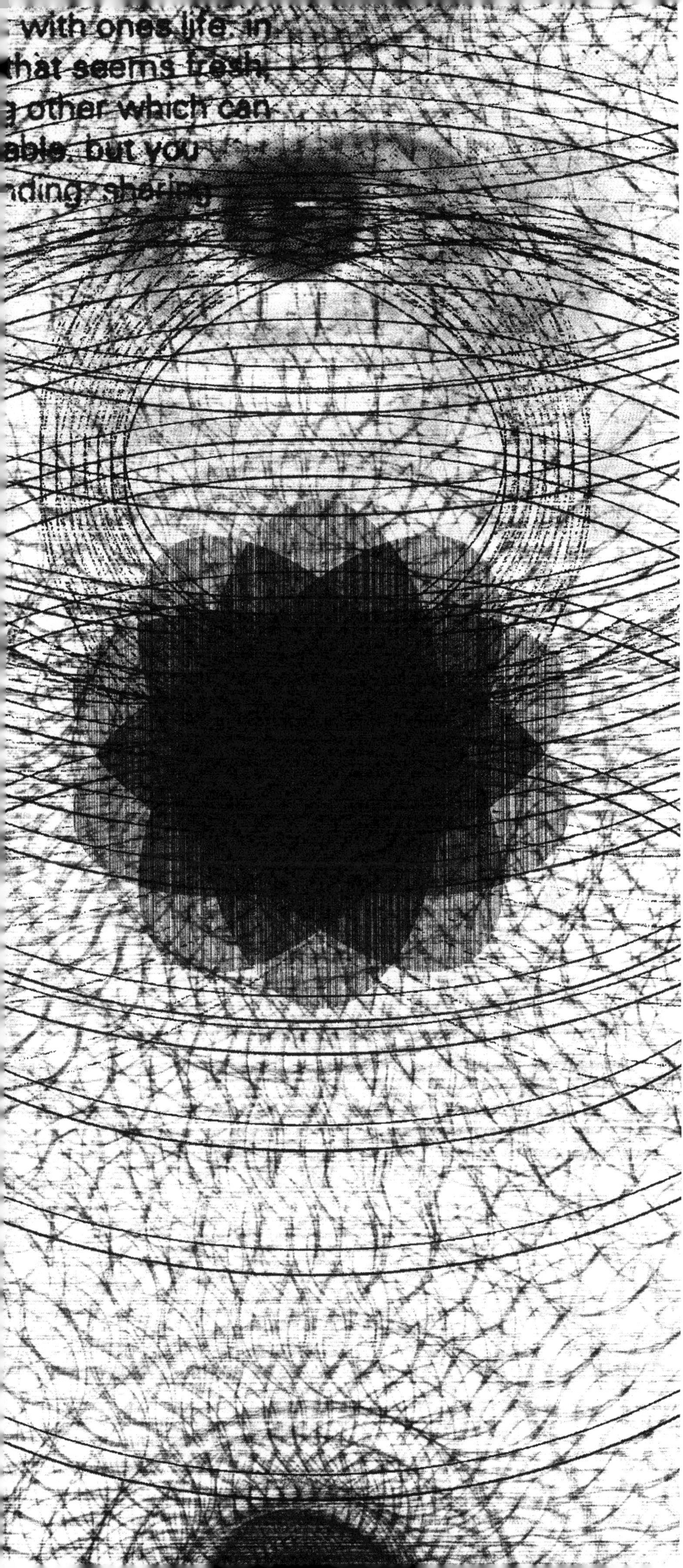

sibi
ing,
h . .
a st
on . .
on c

e in

k of
t. It

k al
spir

is v
ctua
qua
nne
gs
ed-
cep
sedu

We very rarely, if at all, say, or express, the notion that the experience was of no consequence whatsoever: that we learnt nothing from it: that it was an entirely neutral event.

sibility, starting
ing, animating,
h . . . numerical
a state of mind,
on . . .
on of what comes next.

in all its twisted and intertwining forms

of global love and joy
t. It is pure
y of being just

eriences it and
k about gossip,
spiration,

Nerve-shattering!
Energy Blasts!
Power!
Imagination!
Gravity!

YOU ARE NOT ALONE!

Unlearning! Deconditioning your birth!
Forgetting your name! Going naked!

is very very important-being open to chance thr
ection . . . my tendency is to set up a very fixed
ctually no different really to any other approach
re playing . . (conceptual approaches) but withi
way getting external influences (the weather, h
e process.
quality and
se what I'm seeing. Literally. Music alter
e street, twice, with headphones, and listen to
nness and
events to galvanise the physical and emotiona
me, from conception to memory, experience its
gs one does, and
en themes (concept, tool, objective) in most co
responds with another concept, an
ed-ness . . . the closed, internal loop) in a
what you will, the loop is a construct that mani

ceptual terms, how do we explore the aesthetic
seductive and

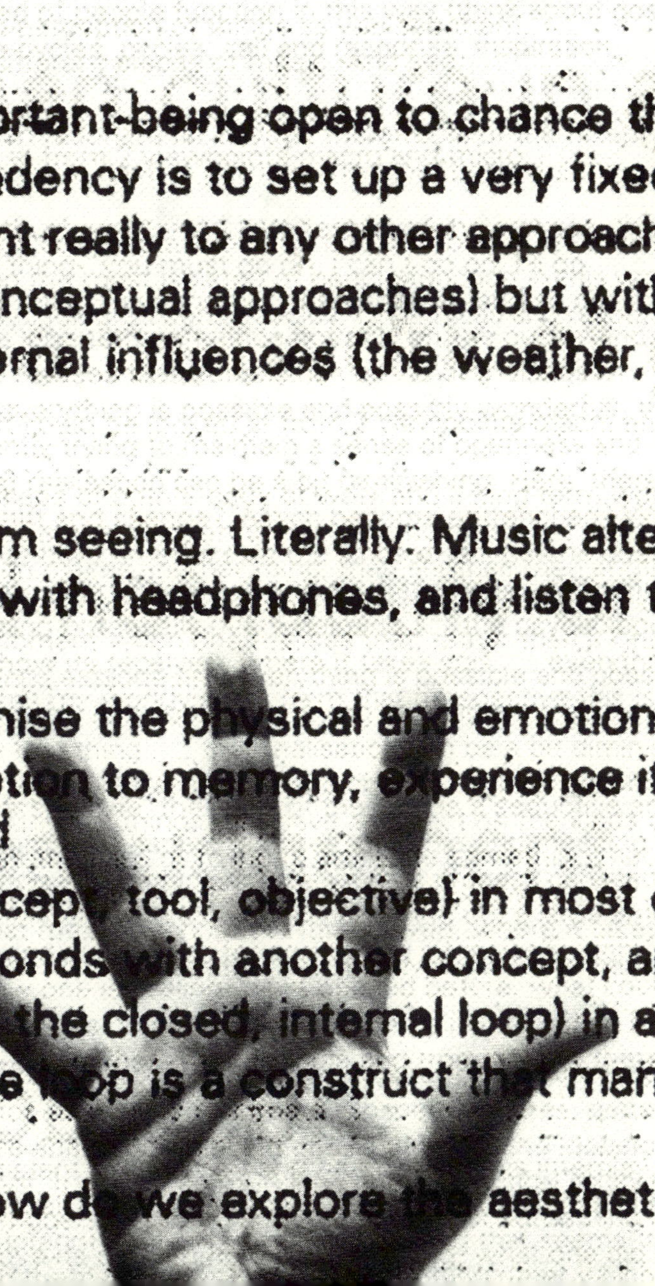

From this perspective, in the attempt to describe the whole sequence (for the moment, removing the qualities of experience, the good or bad or neutral)

together then why? what nourishment is gained by clawing onto other's shoulders distracted and consumed by the pursuit of title and award? how does it benefit the dream of beautiful things to constrain

THE EXECUTIVE MUST LOOK AT PRESENTATIONS. CHOOSE PICTURES FOR THEM.

it seems
clear that

there are 3
states of

experience —

through the hocus-pocus of inadequacy and fear (both the main attributes and weapons of those who would claim business as their idol) with the myths of perfection, individualism, and problem solving? how

THE EXECUTIVE MUST GO TO MEETINGS.

looking forward (anticipation),

involvement (empeiria),

looking back (anamnesis)—

none of which, of course, can exist without the thing itself.

Together, in a linear sense, these 3 states create a kind of hierarchical flux.

does a list of found objects, beyond the least essential of monetary way-finding (and, again, unless you're Marcel Duchamp—and you're not), equate to great works? how does having others do the handiwork

THE EXECUTIVE MUST ORGANISE MEETINGS, WHICH IS EVEN TRICKIER BECAUSE OF THE PEOPLE.

experience to take up their own hierarchy dependant on the individual users perception of and journey through the experience, the flux. If the hierarchy is

dependent
on individual
experience,
then it is
a poetic
(individual,
interpretive,
emotional)

flux.

constantly
being made.
there's a
constant,
shared,
autonomous
flow, not a
faux sisyphean
make-work
stop/start(up)
with no sense
of reason or
means. things
themselves
are the focus,
their qualities,

However, these

states and

hierarchies
may not
exist in a
linear sense
exclusively.

What if things
are odder
than that?

textures,
meanings, use,
mystery
and
interrelationships.
people live
and work as
people, not
titles, and
hierarchies shift
and change
with need:
recognition
(awards,
interviews,
fame, celebrity)

AND THEN THERE'S THE PEOPLE.

Stranger?

7 Tips For Marketing Your Small Business Online

STONE
HAND
PURIFY
JOIN
ROT
NATURE
FEED
SPIRIT
MULTIPLYING
LOVE
EVERYTHING
PROJECTIO

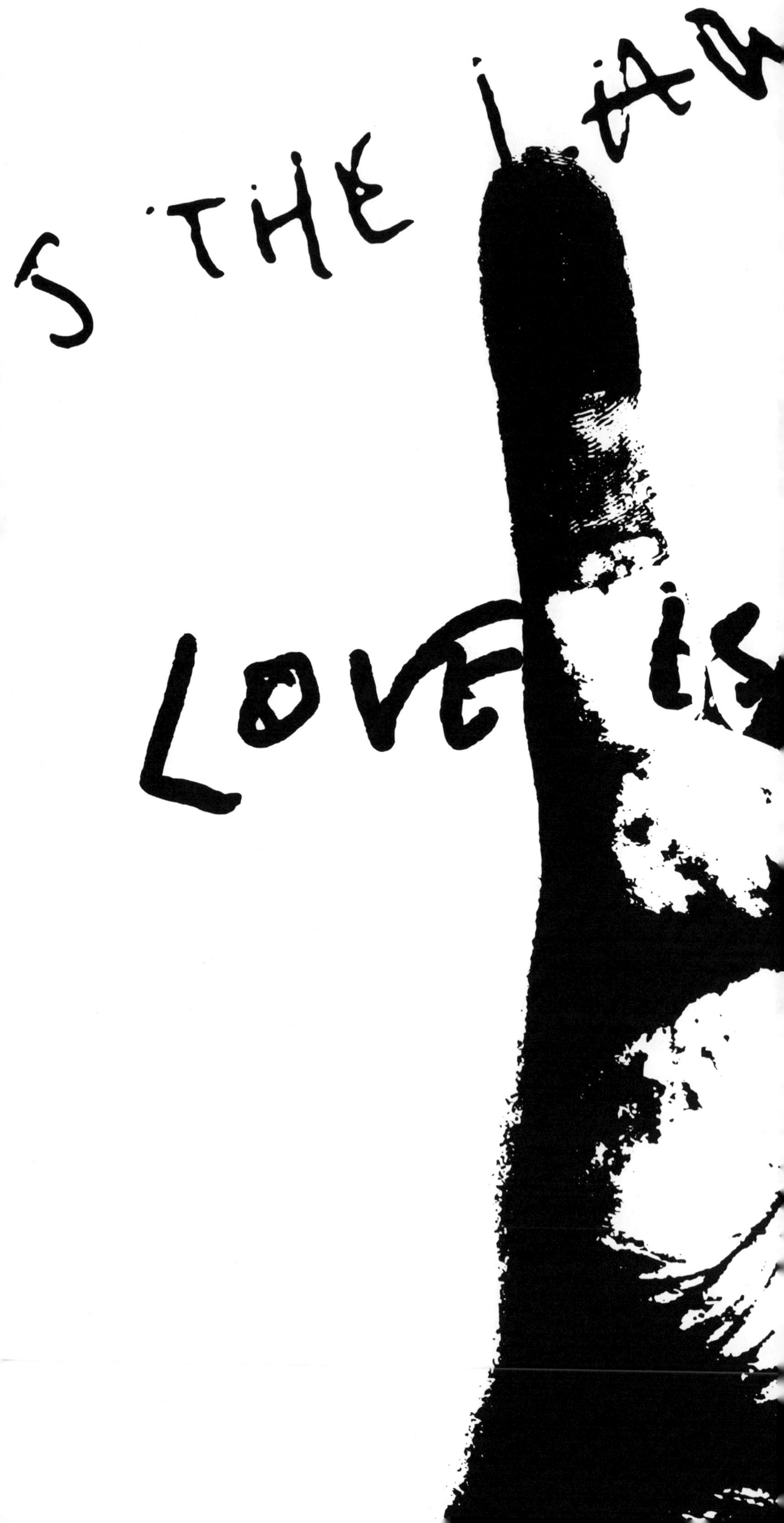
THE
LOVE is

THE LAW

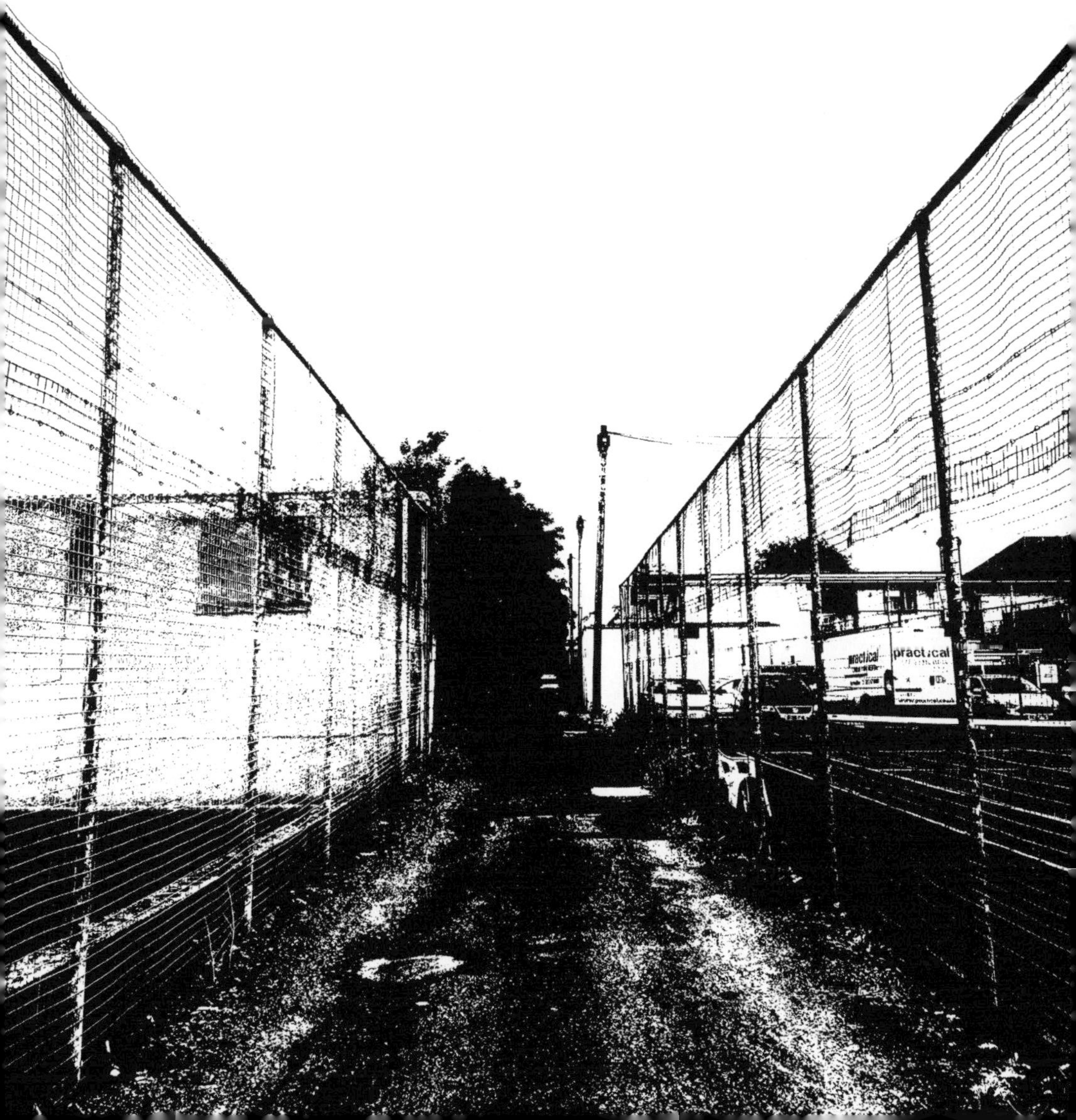
practical
practical

becomes a surprising moment of unexpected joy rather than the pursuit and the object of the whole exercise. if things are never really started, but are in the cycle of perpetual rebirth, then control is impossible.

If any experience could be said to happen in a place,

THE PEOPLE.

then the place where experience happens the longest is the most important environment to consider, and the place where experience

ultimately
and mainly
resides is in
the memory.

perhaps this,
for some,
is the most
frightening
thing.

the things will
escape: this
is the point.
no more
control: out
in the world,
either lost
and ignored
or affecting
causing

ALWAYS WITH A DILEMMA, A BOTHERATION, A HITCH, A HEADACHE, A WORRIMENT, A PICKLE, A CAN OF WORMS.

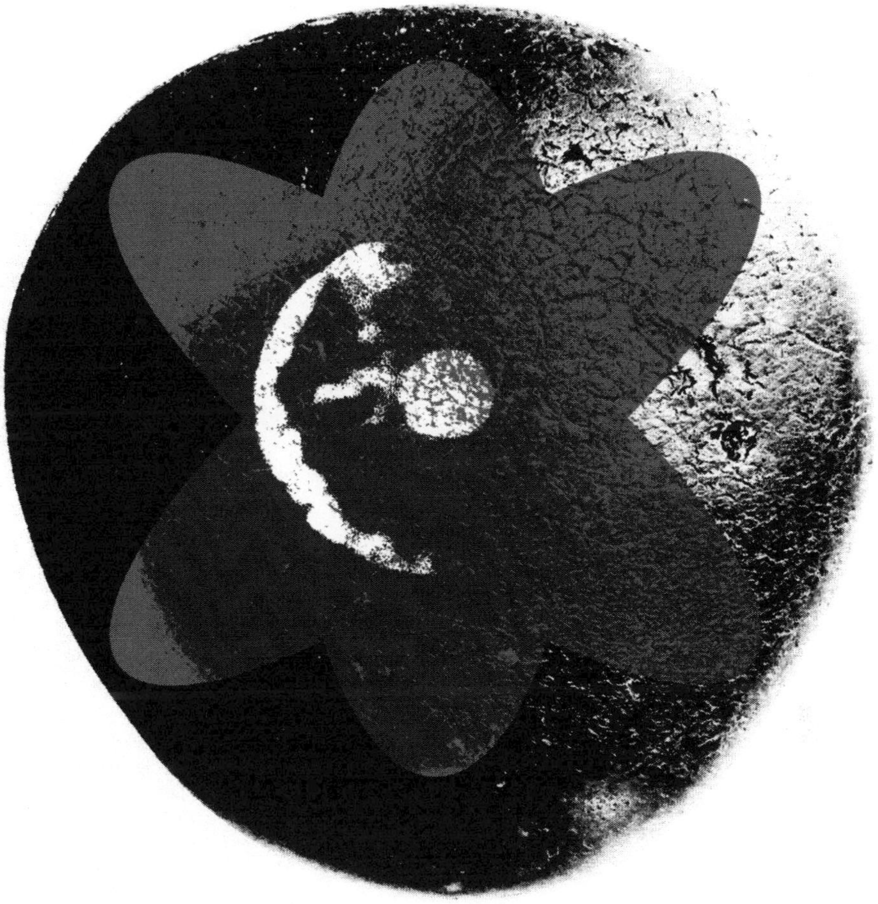

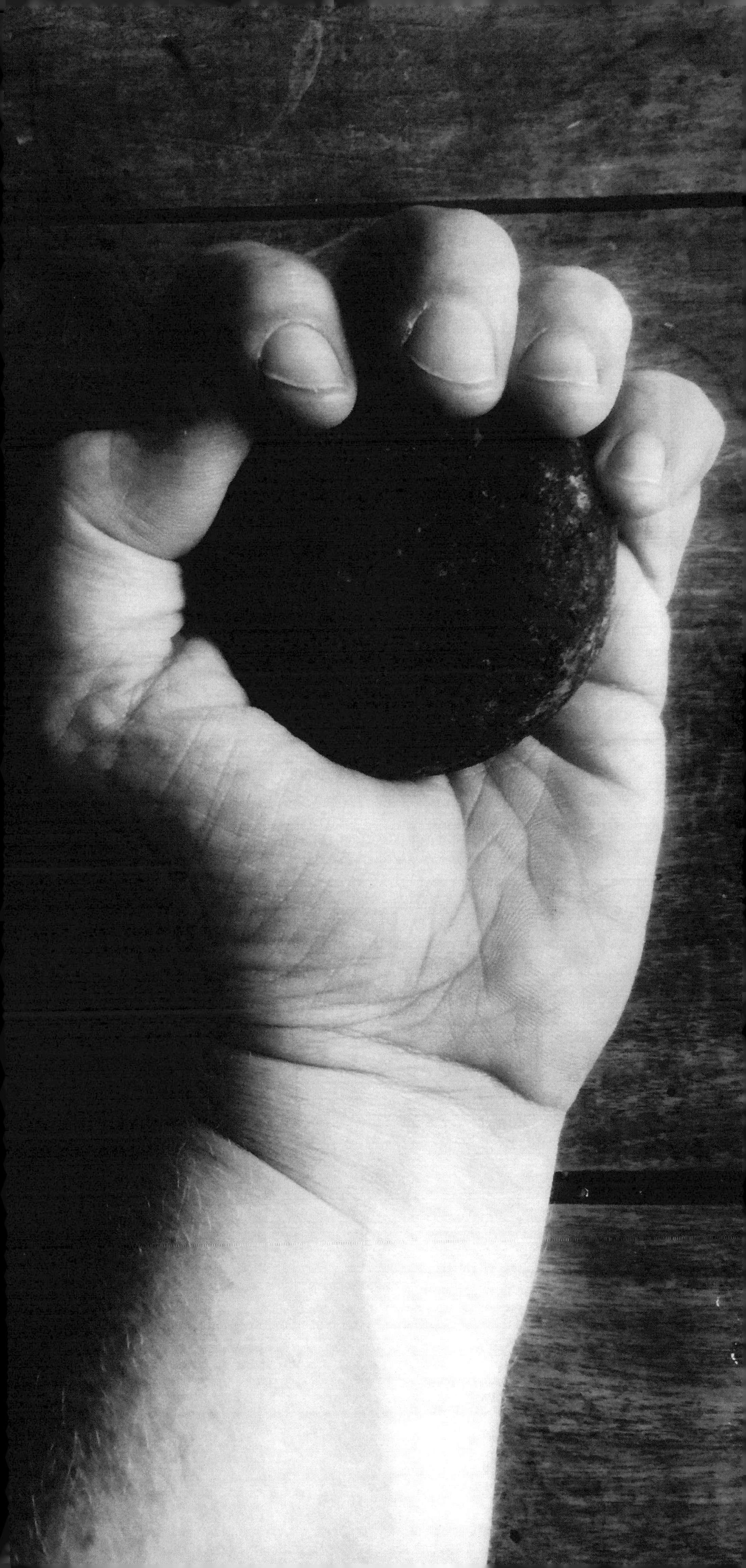

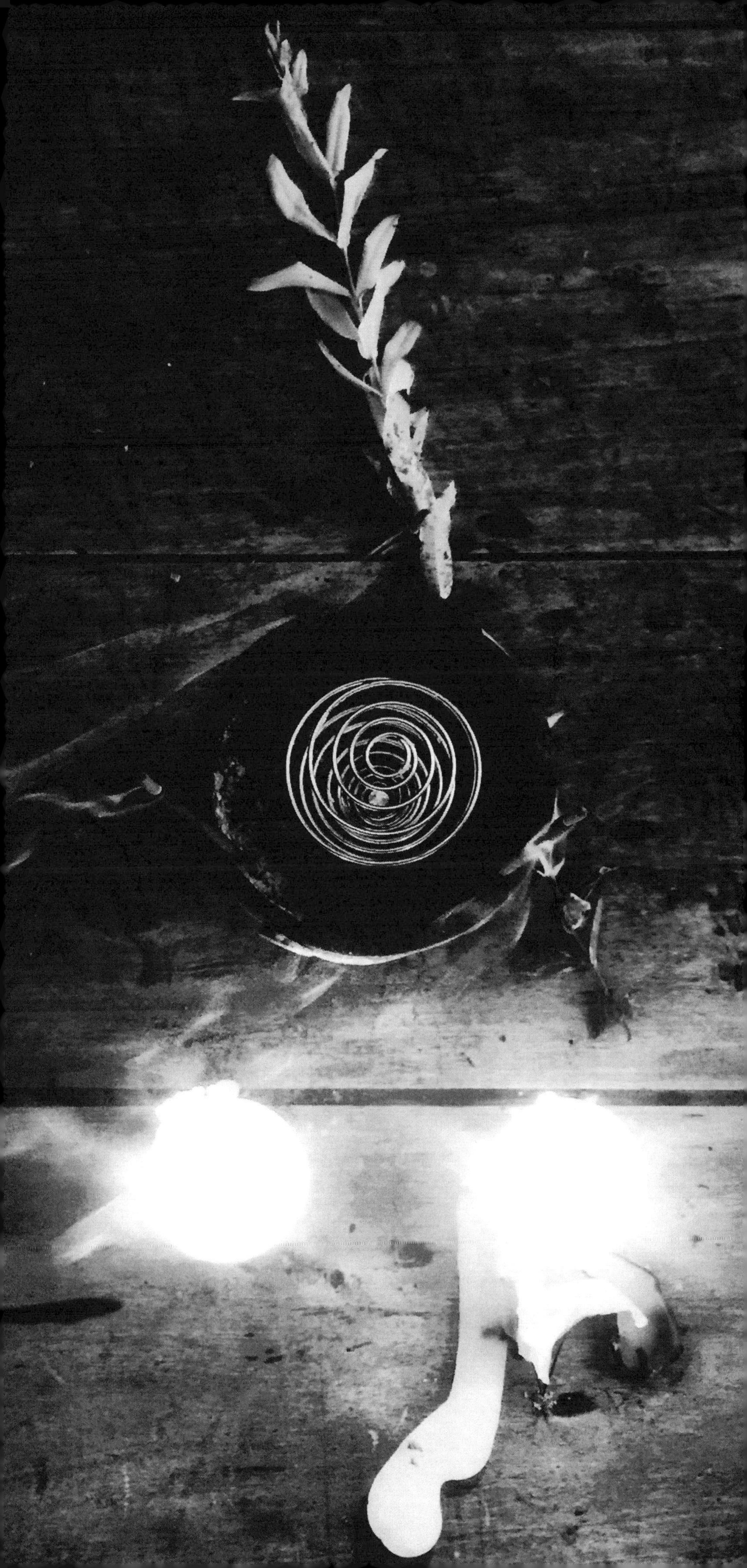

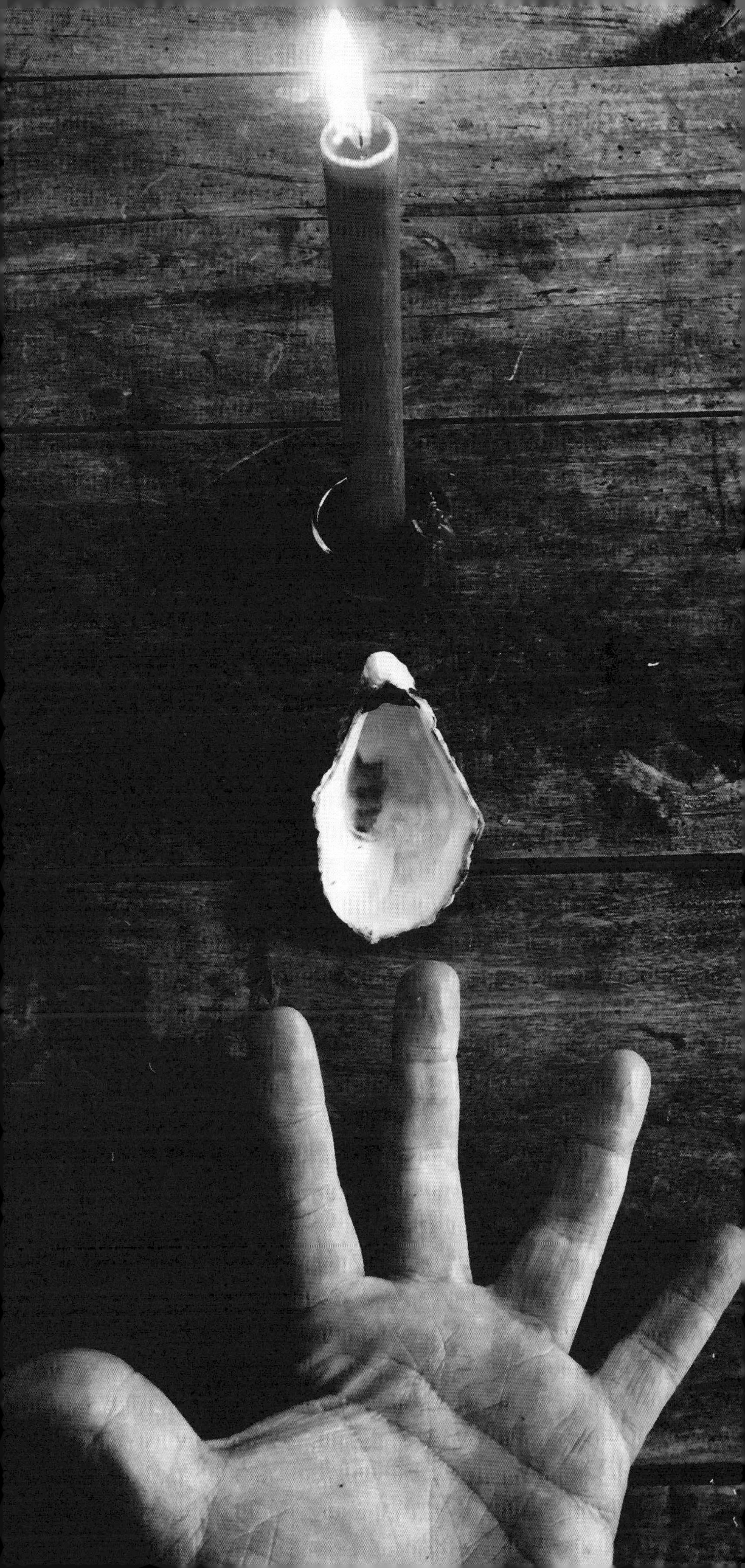

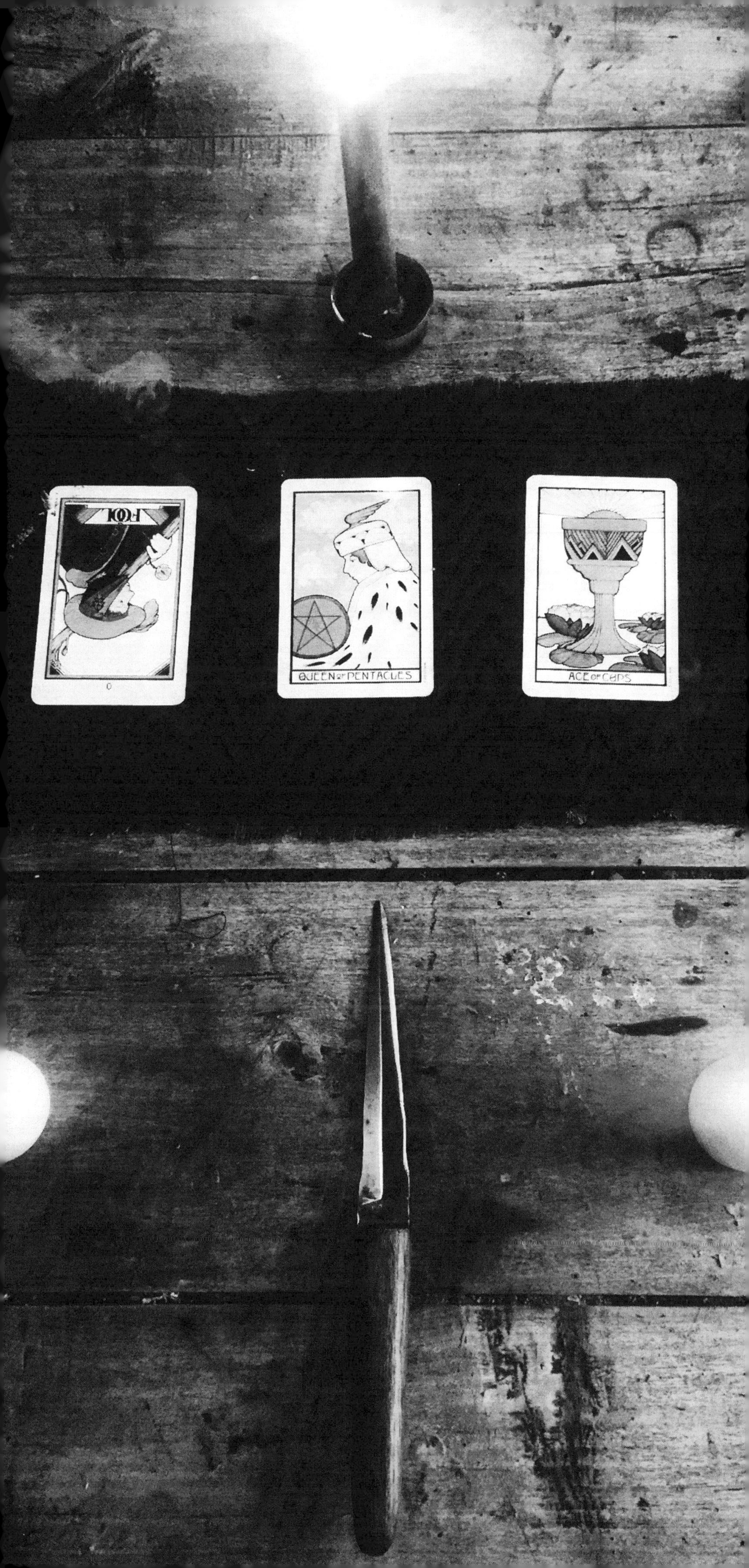
QUEEN of PENTACLES
ACE of CUPS

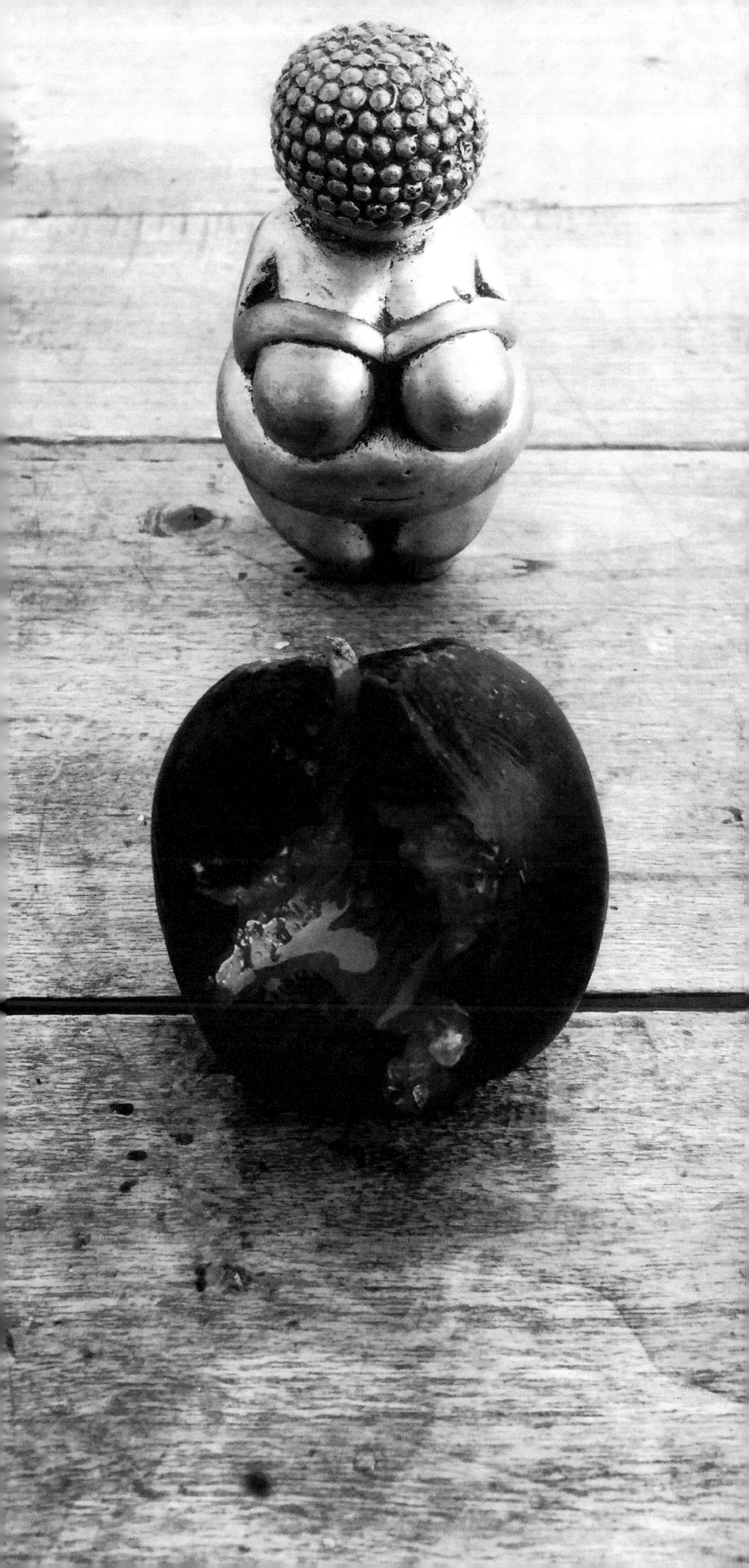

The
natur
exper
is und

of

ence

anny.

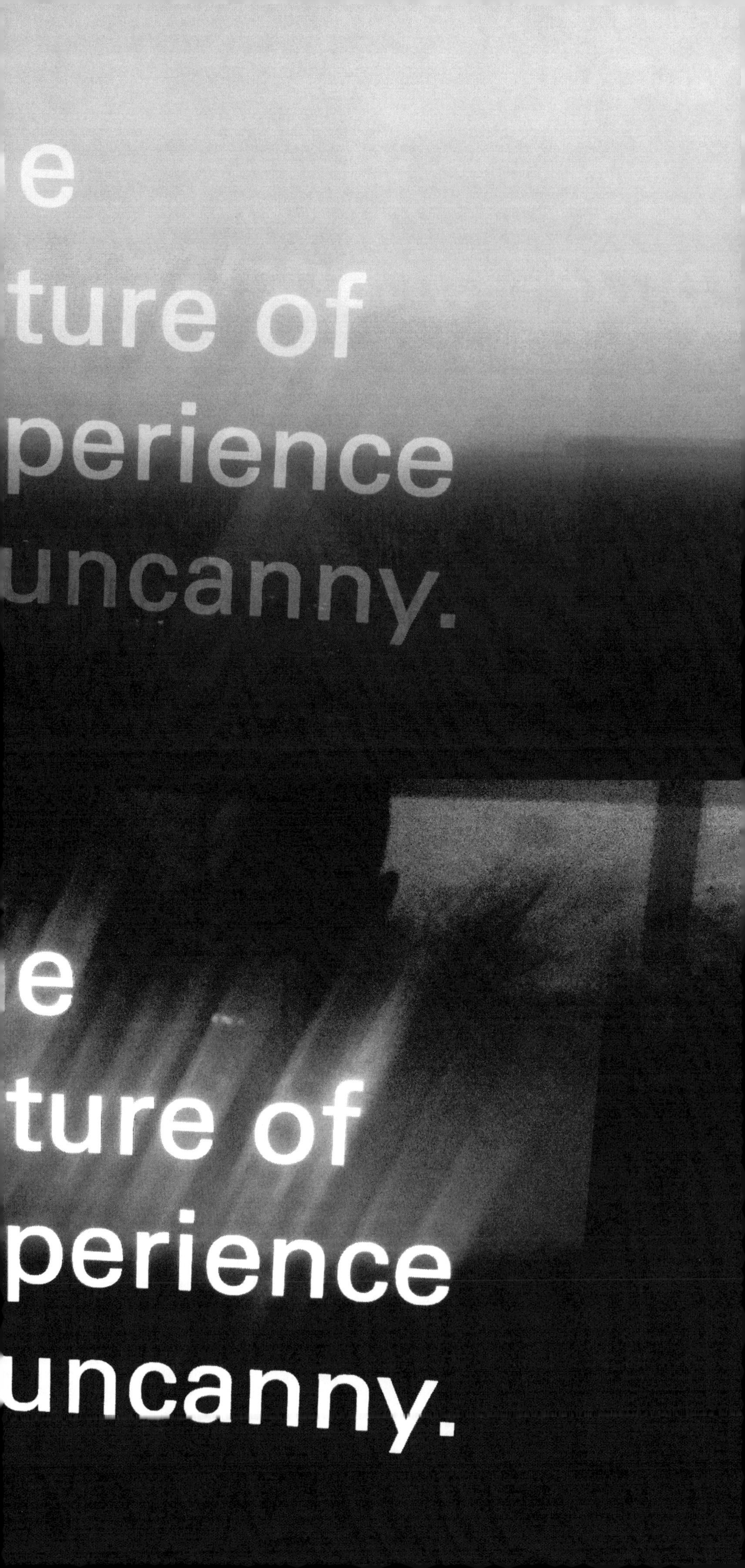
e
ture of
perience
uncanny.
e
ture of
perience
uncanny.

The nature of experience is uncanny.

The nature of experience is uncanny.

Experience
can be
uncanny
because,
as per the
definition
of **uncanny**,
the flux of
experience
tends towards
being familiar
yet strange,

WORMS.

agitating
provoking
causing
changing . . .
if making
things is truly
the point then
it is work and
life and living
and shared,
entwined, and
it will change
and express
and reflect
and embody

which creates
a cognitive
dissonance:
experience,
when residing
in memory, is
at once linear
**(familiar—
the
hierarchical
flux)** and
nonlinear

(strange—the poetic flux).

From the perspective of memory, any experience is in a state of flux. What is recalled most vividly can change from reminiscence

emotion thought idea: it will infuse with empathy reveal possibility achieve illumination bring to life enable engage inspire explode

THE EXECUTIVE SIGHS.

to
reminiscence,
the suggested
categories
oscillating
each other
even to the
point of
a kind of
multiplication
of state upon
state, with

even the possibility of memory itself becoming part of the flux.

In essence, the states are always changing place, yet remain

THE EXECUTIVE IS FLUSTERED.

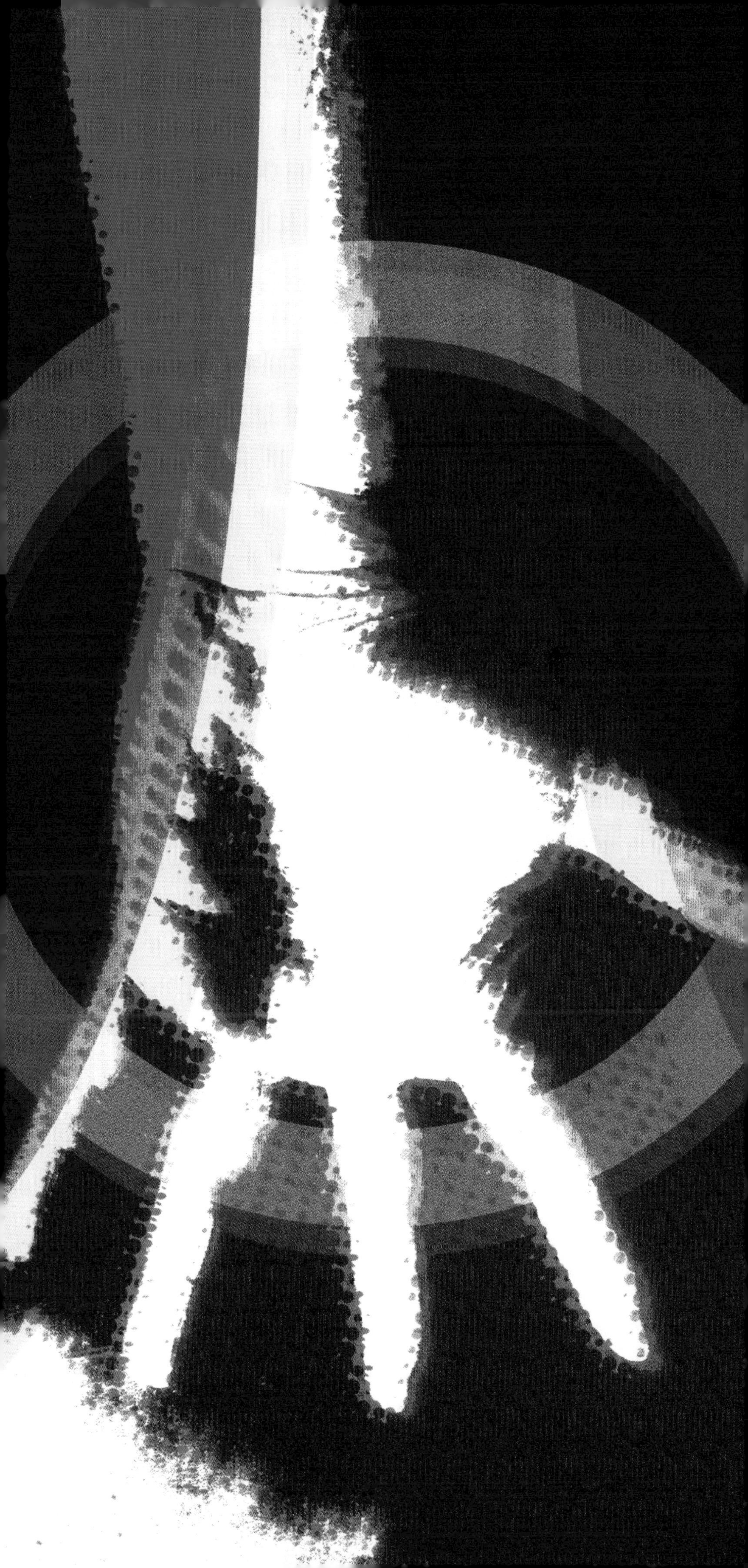

hierarchically organised.

By this point, the thing itself has become the experience, and vice versa—even in the first instance, from

Serendipity. Which is very very important-being open to chance throughout the process . . . or even more so, being open to change, possibility, starting again, changing direction . . . my tendency is to set up a very fixed sequence of events (thinking, writing, making imagery, shooting, editing, animating, post . . . which is actually no different really to any other approach to moving image, except possibly some of the tools I use to work with . . . numerical systems, grids, game playing . . . conceptual approaches) but within that to interefere, subvert, conceptualise, freeform, play and so on. a state of mind, a philosophical pathway; letting external influences (the weather, how one feels, interruption, distraction, focus, time of day and on and on . . .) affect the work, the process.

this vantage point, the notion that the thing itself is of primary importance (the prime mover) is in recession—so the state of the thing alters too, as the

experience unfolds.

When I listen to music I see what I'm seeing. Literally. Music alters the resonance / perception of things as you see them. Walk down the same street, twice, with headphones, and listen to 2 completely different pieces of music. And see.

"A person's life purpose is nothing more than to rediscover, through the detours of art or love or passionate work, those one or two images in the presence of which the heart first opened."
Albert Camus

tension that causes events to galvanise the physical and emotional reaction that can resonate far beyond the effects of the 'fixed' object. It is pure process at every point, from conception to memory, experience itself, and experience in itself is perhaps the most powerful thing in life. It is life.

IT'S ALL JUST SO MUCH . . . WORK.

The 'loop' is a prevalent theme (concept, tool,

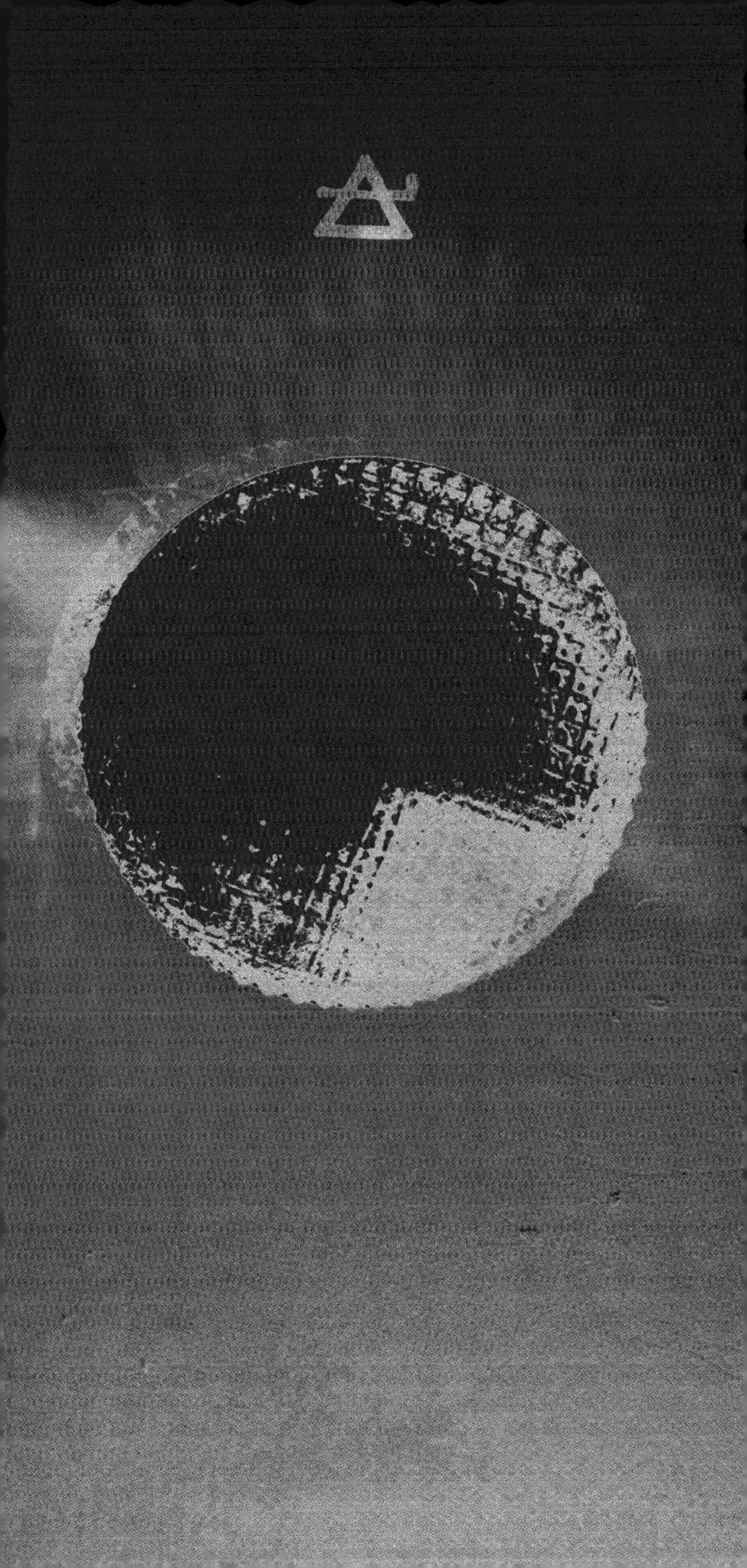

6) The experience of transformation

The notion of memory as a medium, like poetry or film, in concert with the act of 'opening up' offers us a very simple, self-sustaining and almost infinitely rich art form, the story. All you need is yourself, to start with. This is elegant. It is beautiful. However, so far we have a medium (memory) and the act (to remember and to tell).

What is the

EFFORT.

objective) in most communications; a concept is executed and distributed, an audience experiences it and responds, the originator in turn responds with another concept, and so on . . . even the most isolated of people function in this way (think about gossip, or—even more isolated— neuroses . . . the closed, internal loop) in a philosophical/ psychological sense— cycles, circles, call and response, inspiration, influence . . . call it what you will, the loop is a construct that manifests everywhere.
So, with these conceptual terms, how do we explore the aesthetic of the 'loop'? it could be looked at from 2 viewpoints—macro and micro.

In the macro sense, and if we can allow the notion of 'aesthetics' to include the shape of both a body of work and a long term working process, there is one sense in which the

subject?

In this case, just as Robert Graves in The White Goddess saw poetry as "... a magical language bound up with popular religious ceremonies in honor of the moongoddess, or muse, some of them dating from the old stone age, and that this remains the language of true poetry..." —in essence,

arguably that **the**

subject of

loop looms large. This is in the process of a lifes work, the Samuel Beckett thing—"you must go on, I can't go on, I'll go on." —which can allude to the sheer joy/enormity of how one makes something, then makes another thing, then another, then another and so on. This is the looping effort of a working life, and in the broad sense of aesthetics here it comes into play as a long-term influence not only on the quality and quantity of work, but also on the ability and desire to do it in the first place. The moment when one realises that, rather than a kind of mélange of seemingly chaotic, energising and joyful experiences (when things start, when things explode and everything is possible and possibly wonderful), the actuality is of doing it (whatever 'it' is) again and again and again and again (until death!) and constantly trying

KEEPING UP.

poetry is the adoration of the feminine

muse, the goddess with many names—or as Tarkovsky saw film, "the infinite cannot be made into matter, but it is possible to create an illusion of the infinite: the image." Here, i wonder; does memory have a subject?

Can it?

Is it possible?

Or desirable?

Perhaps as a means towards envisioning a way to be, can one be imagined and conjured? For good reasons—towards making things that are open, compassionate, human, active—can a useful subject be inferred in order to create a spark, a moment's consideration that sharpens focus in a way that encourages communication, encourages doing things, brings to life; as Sottsass said, "just feel what it's like to do things by trying to do them, trying to find out whether everyone can do things, other things, with their hands or machines — or whatever — etcetera etcetera. Can it be tried? My friends say it can."

WITH TRENDS AND INSIGHTS AND TECHNOLOGY AND JUST ALL THAT STUFF.

Can it be tried?

8 Ways to Win the Race for Creative Talent

to maintain a sense of openness and curiousness and allowing oneself to be inspired and all of that as if it were the very first thing . . . that realisation can be a bit diminishing. Here, there is a loop of rhythm and pattern in its largest sense—as one grows older, what rhythms, which patterns shift and change? Which become entrenched? Which are discovered to be irrelevant, immature, or damaging? Over time, these are the kinds of things that have an effect on the kinds of things one does, and the reasons for doing them. This is somewhat woolly I think, but has a bearing nonetheless—I'm trying to articulate something that is a feeling to me, like a weather system . . . how that affects your day and can add up beyond the immediate into something potentially overwhelming . . . the psychological effects of it, the questioning of it

The sub
memor
the
experie
transfor

ect of

is

nce of

mation.

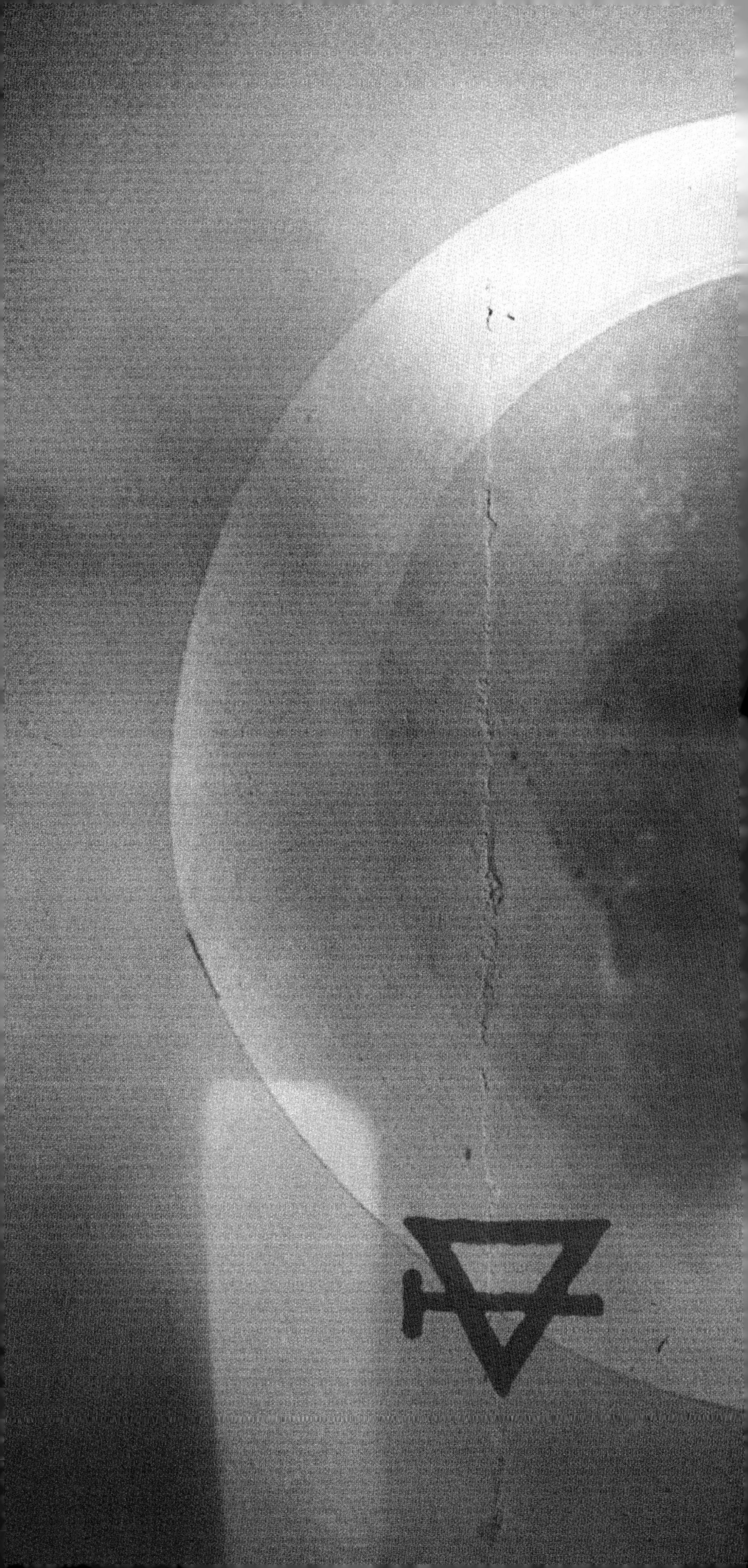

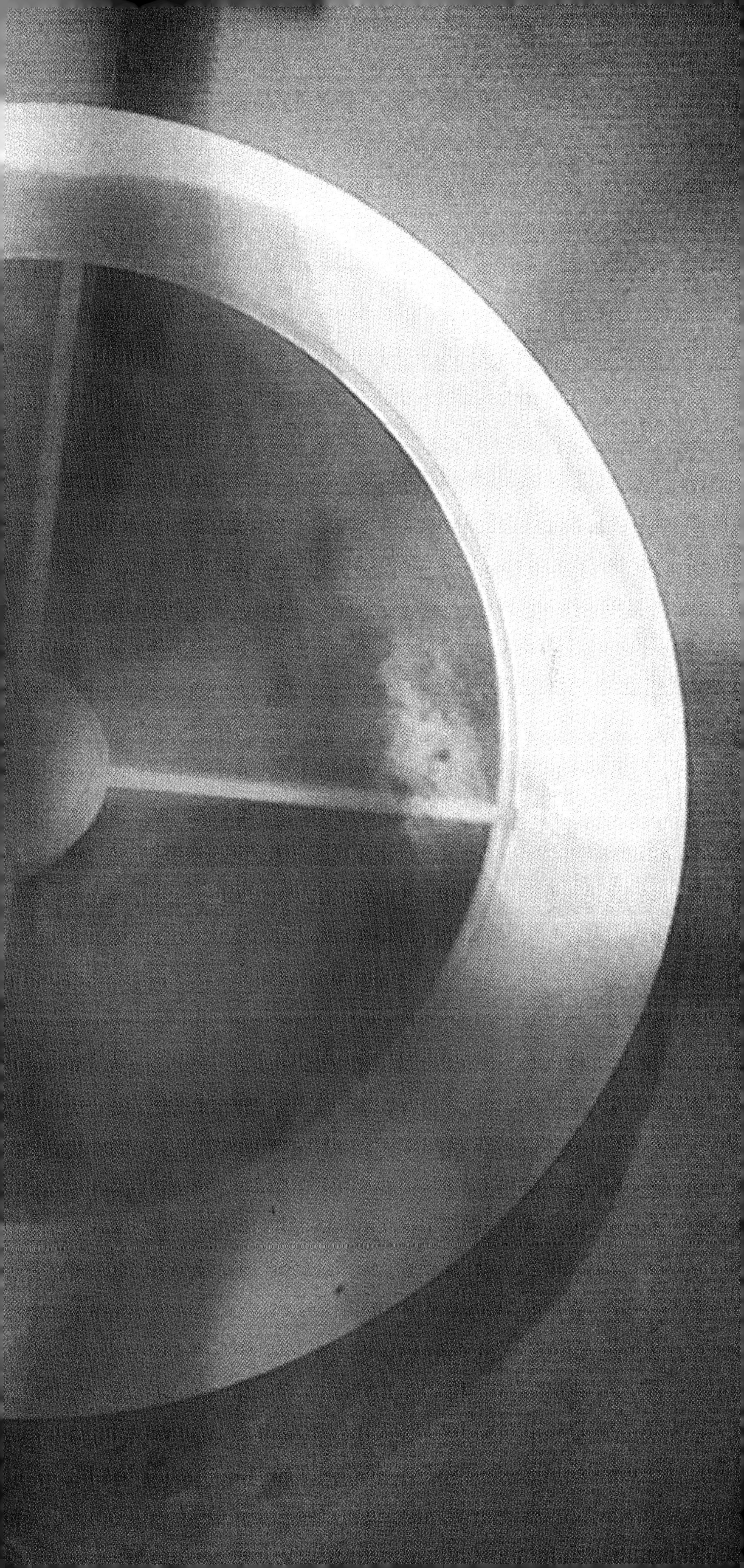

SAMHAIN Circle

Earth
Air
Fire
Water

3 Sheaves Bread
5 Candles Wine

The things a person has lived through that have changed them somehow. To recount the impressions of metamorphosis. Any works created through the medium of memory and the act of recounting have as their subject the experience of transformation.

Good, bad, big, small, vivid, faded, melancholy, ecstatic . . .

IT SEEMS THAT PEOPLE DO THESE THINGS JUST TO MAKE THE EXECUTIVE FEEL UNEASY.

(and by 'it' I mean what one does, and for me that means work), how it's received, where it takes you . . . everything. Work has determined my life—I can see that now—and that's the way my life has gone. This means that my worldview is from that perspective—this is where I find myself. I work therefore I am. This is my loop. This is my life.

In the micro sense—the aesthetic of the loop is central to both process and result. From a process perspective, the form of the loop is a seductive and inspiring thing. Through overlay and repetition new forms can be found unlooked-for, as if grown, animate. Shapes, textures, patterns and meaning emerge out of grids, systems, marks and so on, and by continually analysing and re-analysing, thinking and re-thinking, the looping process can lead into unknown territory, which is good. It may

Telling, showing, sharing to understand and build. To develop mind and feeling. To know how another feels and to understand and to modify behaviour (in line with the golden rule) because of that understanding in order for humanity to take its next steps.

Because we cannot and must not ever stop asking Gaugin's question—

1) with unconditional love

”Where do we come from?

sound intense or complex, but often its not. It can be as mundane and as practical as laying out a large amount of type on a grid, or as effortless as daydreaming, but the looping activity is what triggers the mind and eye to look for something intrinsically ‘right’. This notion of ‘right’ (aesthetically) is entwined with the macro viewpoint I describe above—it’s to do with how one is feeling, what one did before, what could be happening next, and so on. All loops within loops, constantly feeding back. Eno’s concept of looping overlays creating ‘moiré’ patterns is interesting here, because its in the moiré that you find what you’re looking for (and sometimes literally it’s a moiré!), somewhere in the tangle and trompe l’oeil there can be a glint of something that implies a whole picture, a suggestion, a moment . . . Both consciously and

What are we?

2) an interaction deeper than collaboration

Where are we going?"

unconsciously, influence is like circles on circles, spirals. From nearby and constant, to faraway and rare, there's this interplay that shifts and changes over time but never disappears. Cause and effect, ebb and flow, give and take . . . all contributing to what one does with one's life. in this sense, everything becomes 'both/and'; by this I mean that there are moments of quiet and exploration that might result in a thing that seems fresh, unrecognised . . . and there are times of play, collaborating, taking 2 unconnected things and putting them together to make something other which can feel unproductive . . . and vice versa . . . and so on, back and forth. Total influence, as much and as often as possible. Not only unavoidable, but you wouldn't want to avoid it—it should be encouraged, sought out, nurtured, enabled

3) working with composite and associative modes of thought

A drift : lost on a beach .
A different beach

Changing — cold morning
Kites along the ecliptic rising

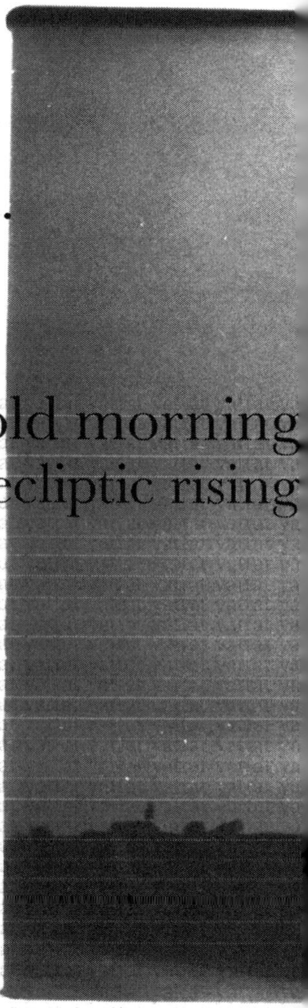

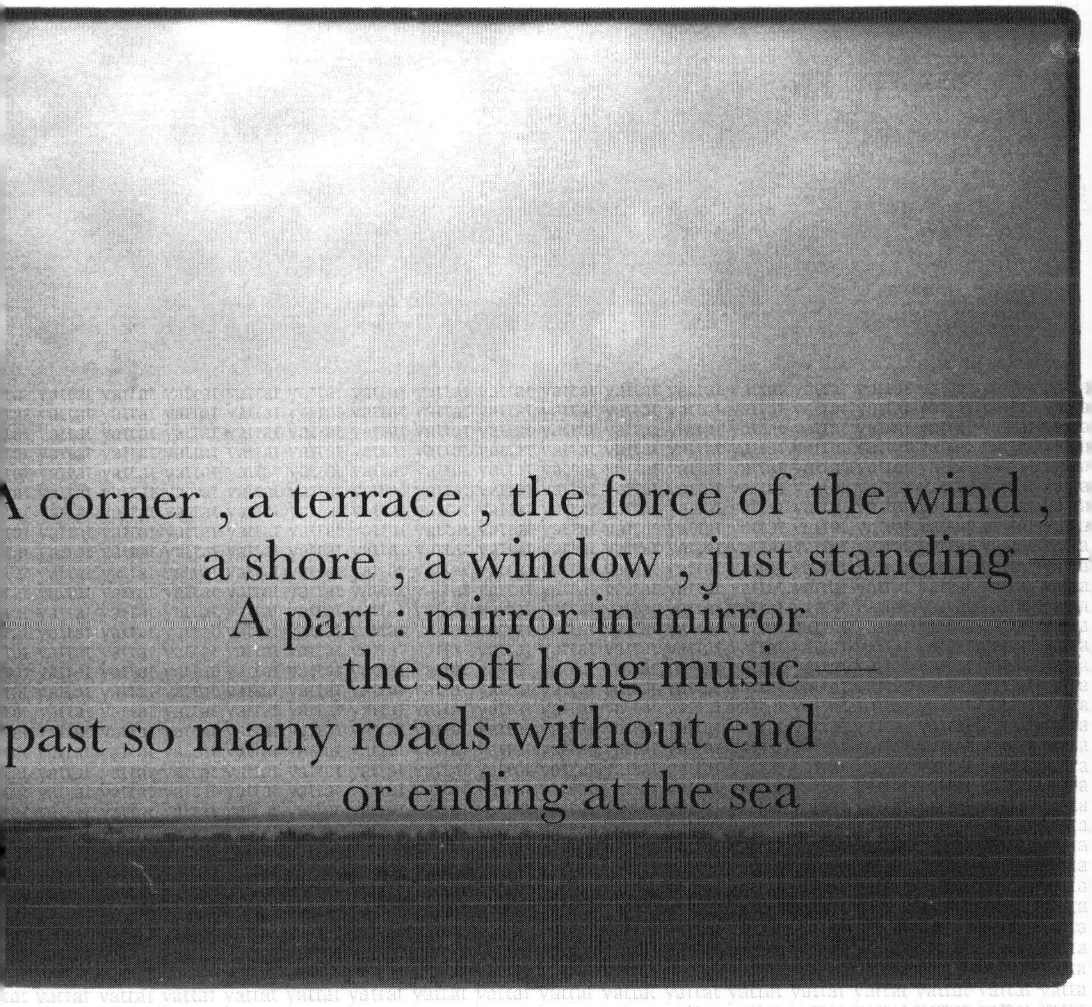

A corner , a terrace , the force of the wind ,
a shore , a window , just standing —
A part : mirror in mirror
the soft long music —
past so many roads without end
or ending at the sea

7) The golden rule

Do what you say you'll do.

Respond in good time with grace.

If you ask for something and it happens, take the time to appreciate

THEY DO THEM DELIBERATELY.

and acknowledge what's been done.

to flourish. Contact—collaboration, that close understanding, sharing between people—ultimately, it is the work, the life.

Always communicate.

"A way shall be found before a why shall be found." Brian Eno

Explain reasons.

10 TIPS FOR ASPIRING DIGITAL MARKETERS

If you make a mistake, make the effort to fix it as fast as you can.

4) filled with compelling purpose

Use the golden rule (from wikipedia):

China

Zi gong asked, saying, "is there one word that may serve as a rule of practice for all one's life?" The master said, "is not reciprocity such a word?"
Confucius

"Never impose on others what you would not choose for yourself."
Confucius

"If people regarded other people's families in the same way that they regard their own, who then would incite their own family to attack that of another? For one would do for others as one would do for oneself."
Mozi

"The sage has no interest of his own, but takes the interests of the people as his own. He is kind to the kind; he is also kind to the unkind: for virtue is kind. He is faithful to the faithful; he is also faithful to the unfaithful: for virtue is faithful."
Laozi

"Regard your neighbour's gain as your own gain, and your neighbour's loss as your own loss."
Laozi

Egypt

"Now this is the command: do to the doer to cause that he do thus to you."

"That which you hate to be done to you, do not do to another."

10 HOTTEST DIGITAL CREATIVE JOBS

Greece

"Do not do to your neighbor what you would take ill from him."
Pittacus

"Avoid doing what you would blame others for doing."
Thales

5) in order to merge the incommensurable

"What you do not want to happen to you, do not do it yourself either."
Sextus the Pythagorean

"Do not do to others what would anger you if done to you by others."
Isocrates

"What thou avoidest suffering thyself seek not to impose on others."
Epictetus

"It is impossible to live a pleasant life without living wisely and well and justly (agreeing 'neither to harm nor be harmed', and it is impossible to live wisely and well and justly without living a pleasant life."
Epicurus

". . . it has been shown that to injure anyone is never just anywhere."
Socrates

IN THE OFFICE, A LUNCHTIME MEETING.

Rome

"Expect from others what you did to them."
Seneca

"It is not so, as you might believe, that one is made happy through the unhappiness of others."
Seneca

6) through ordinarily irreconcilable methods of understanding

India

"Hence, (keeping these in mind), by self-control and by making dharma (right conduct) your main focus, treat others as you treat yourself."
Sanskrit

"Why does a man inflict upon other creatures those sufferings, which he has found by experience are sufferings to himself?"
Thiruvalluvar

"Let not a man consent to do those things to another which, he knows, will cause sorrow."
Thiruvalluvar

IT'S AN IMPORTANT MEETING BUT THERE WERE SO MANY SENIOR EMPLOYEES

Humanism

"Do not do to others what you would not want them to do to you."

7) towards a shared vision of potential

Monty Python

"Try and be nice to people, avoid eating fat, read a good book every now and then, get some walking in, and try and live together in peace and harmony with people of all creeds and nations."

THERE THAT THE EXECUTIVE ONLY HAD TO SAY HELLO TO THE MAIN CLIENT AND INTRODUCE EVERYONE BEFORE TUCKING IN TO A LOVELY LIGHT LUNCH.

8) with no unequivocal resolution

9) and an open remit for future, unforeseen contribution

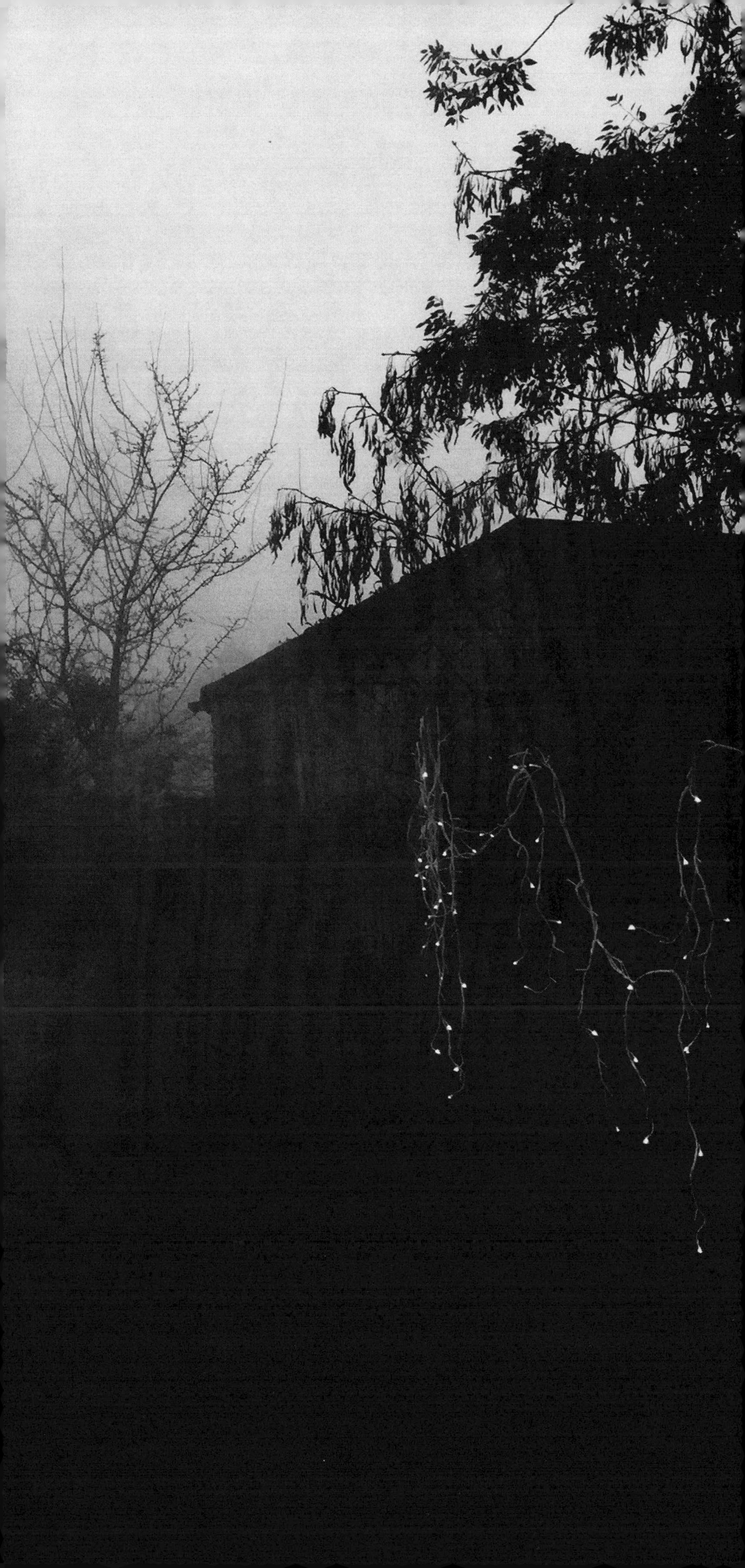

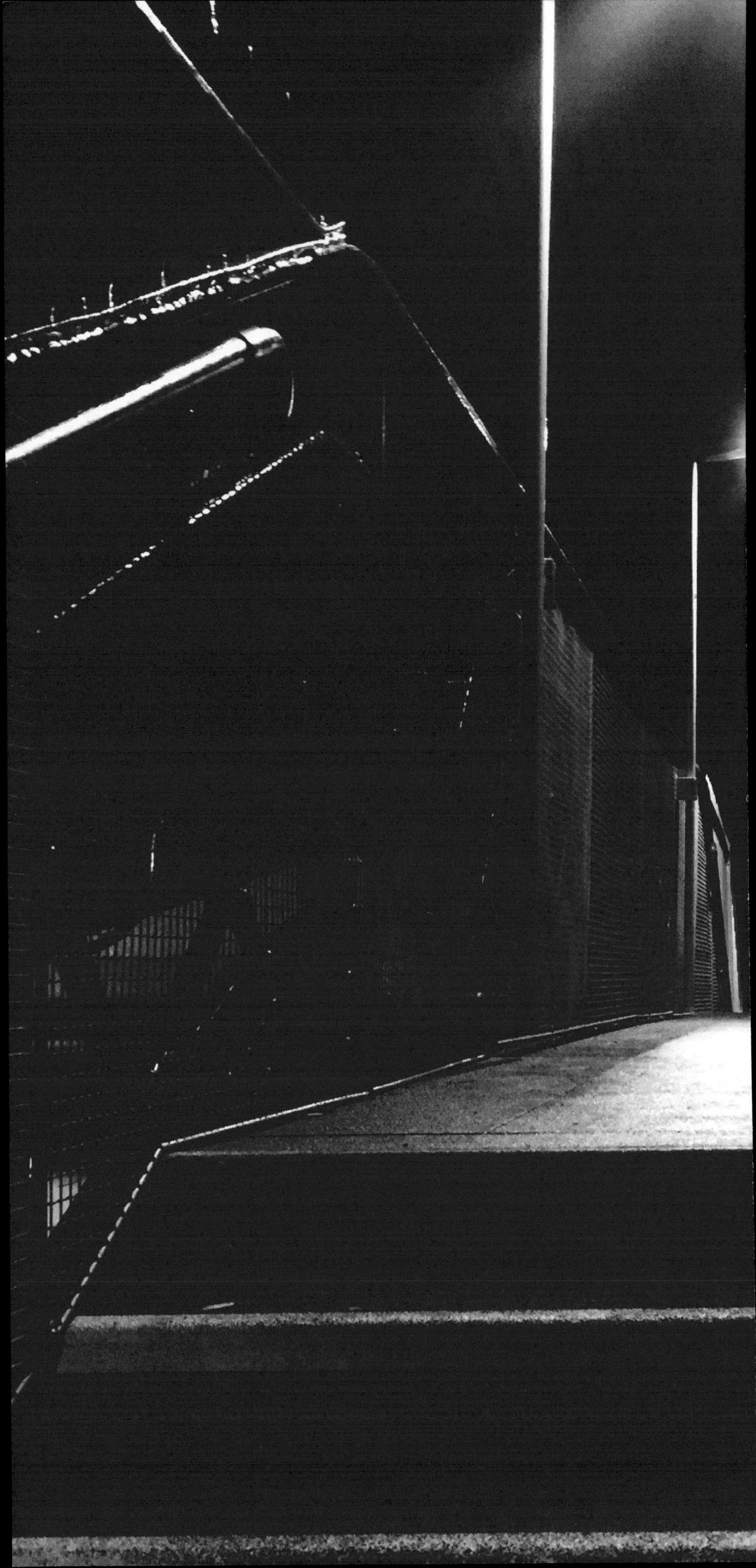

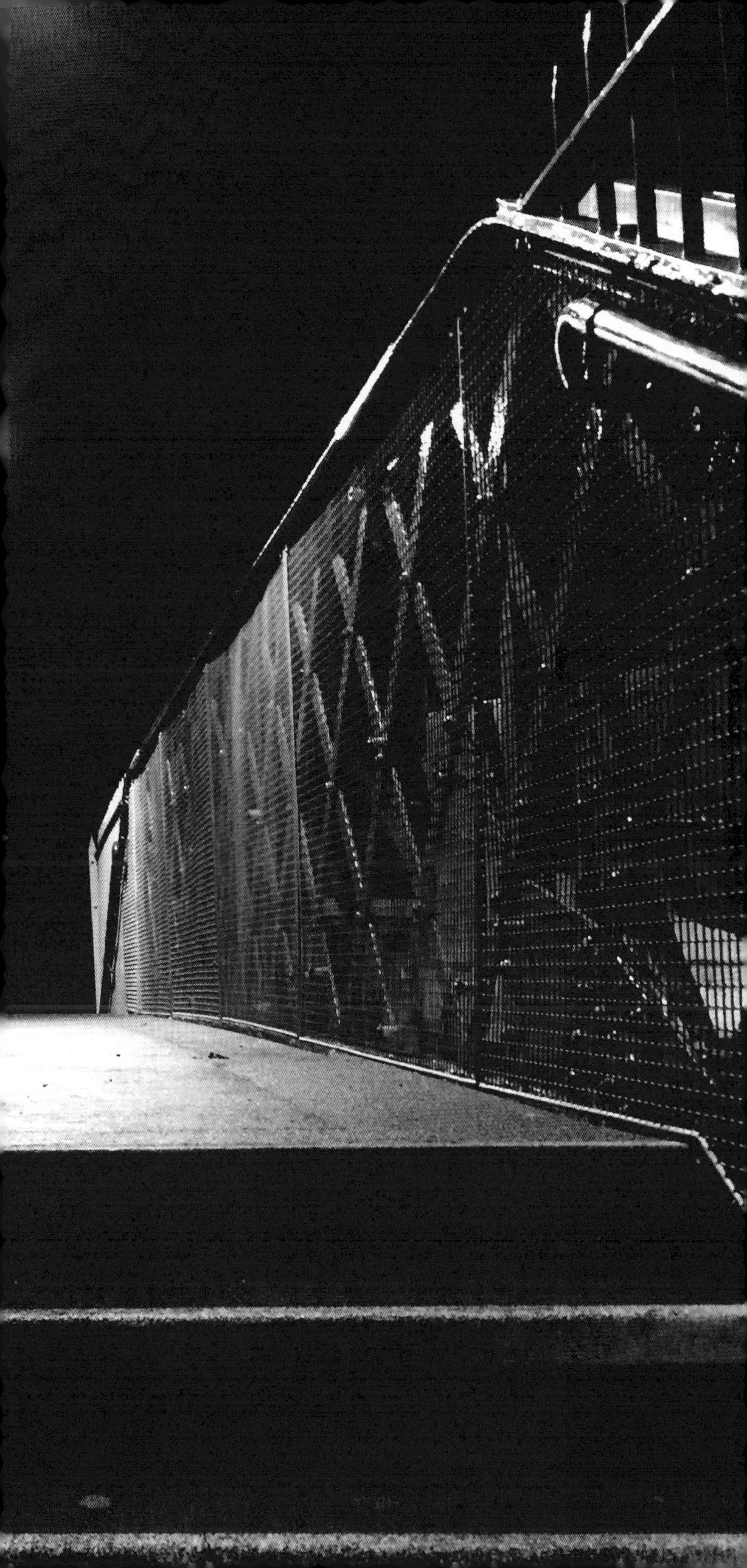

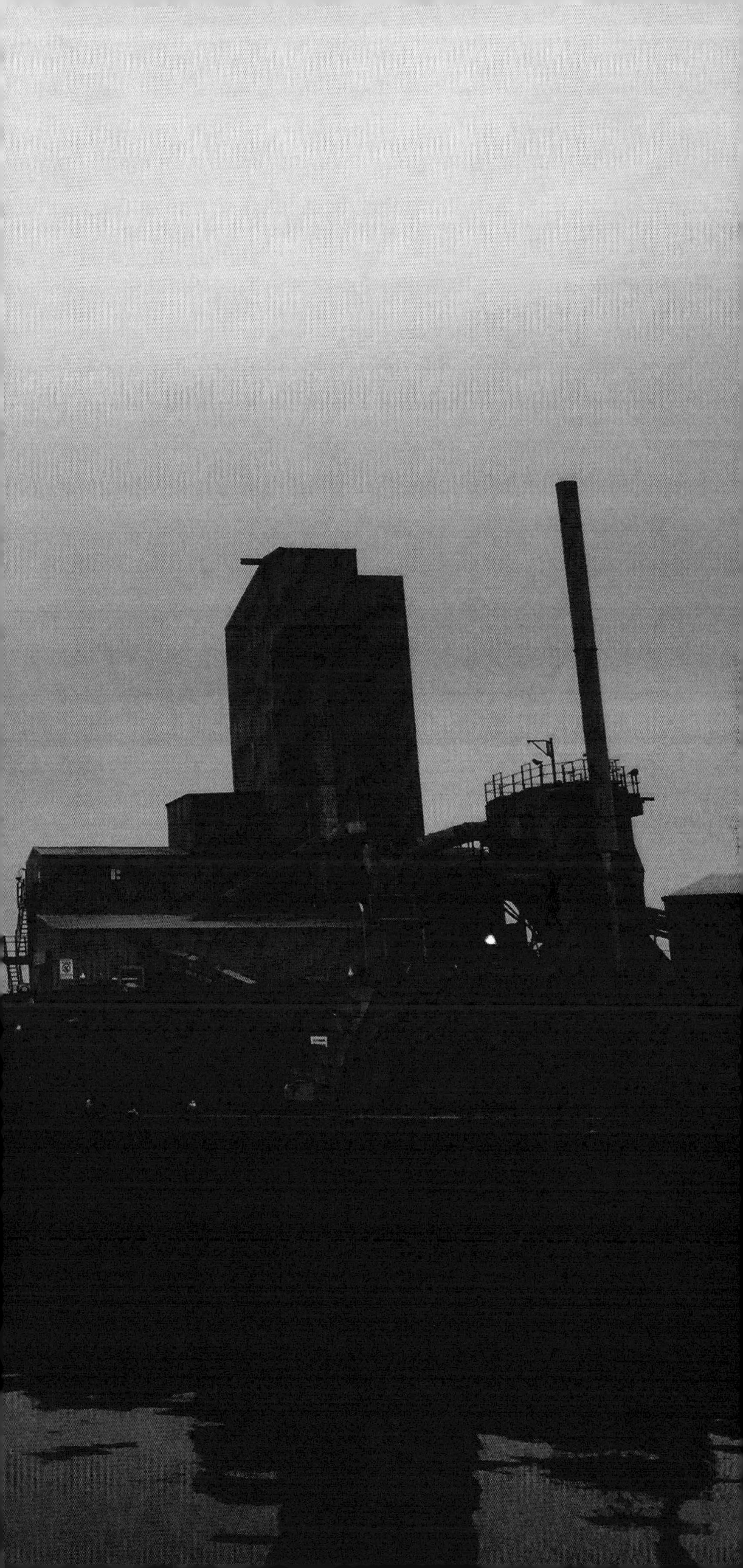